INSPIRATIONAL BASEBALL STORIES FOR YOUNG READERS

12 UNBELIEVABLE TRUE TALES TO INSPIRE AND AMAZE YOUNG BASEBALL LOVERS

Mike Johnson

ISBN: 979-8-89095-001-7

TABLE OF CONTENTS

ATTENTION:

DO YOU WANT MY FUTURE BOOKS AT HEAVY DISCOUNTS AND EVEN FOR FREE?

HEAD OVER TO WWW.SECRETREADS.COM
AND JOIN MY SECRET BOOK CLUB!

INTRODUCTION

Baseball has been considered America's Pastime for over a century because it embodies what makes the country amazing and beautiful. Baseball has helped America cope during periods of great tragedy and pain. Other times, it has led the country in social change and reform. Most importantly, baseball has maintained the power to inspire audiences of any age.

Inspiration occurs during moments of unexpected glory, like a rally at the bottom of the ninth when the game seems unwinnable. It tells us that impossibilities are plausible and if you're determined and work hard enough, dreams are possible.

Nothing is more exciting than an unlikely underdog winning against insurmountable odds. Baseball history is filled with examples of players and teams that did what many others said was an unlikely feat.

However, it is not just these solitary moments that inspire audiences. It is all the steps leading up to the triumph — hard work, commitment, perseverance, and dedication. These lessons apply to everyone, whether you're a young baseball star with a budding career or just a fan looking for inspiration in your daily life.

1

The 12 inspirational baseball stories in this book highlight the many ways athletes push us to do better in our own pursuits. They are examples of outstanding individuals that rose to success in sports and life.

As you read each story, consider the underlying lessons behind these amazing feats and careers. How can you apply these experiences to your life and future baseball endeavors?

The lessons hidden beneath the surface of baseball's best stories are an incredible resource for how to tackle any curveball life throws at you. Without any more delays, let's begin exploring 12 inspirational stories from throughout baseball history.

These stories will lead you to a new understanding of baseball:

CHAPTER 1:

LEARNING TO TIE SHOES AND PITCH A NO-HITTER

Fitting in at a young age is incredibly challenging. Children are constantly concerned with whether or not other kids like them. This same anxiety even haunts many adults. Now imagine you are Jim Abbott in the third grade. You were born with only one hand, adding to the immense pressure of fitting in.

Abbott would hide his prosthetic hand as much as possible, trying not to draw attention to it. This was not from instinct but born out of necessity because the other kids would tease him about it. Some classmates would cry or state that it scared them. One kid flat-out told Abbott he didn't like the prosthetic, as if it was a Scooby Doo lunch box that could easily be changed for a new one.

The worst fear of all was having to tie his shoes. It was one of the things he couldn't do on his own; another painful reminder that he would always be different from his peers. His mother would do her best to tie the shoes tightly each morning.

If they came undone during the day, a teacher would have to tie the laces for him, a spectacle that drew jokes and sneers from classmates, making the young Abbott feel as tall as the shoelaces he couldn't tie were thin. Donn Clarkson, Abbott's third-grade teacher, picked up on this shameful ritual and decided to find a solution for the boy.

As an adult, Abbott tells the story of how he got to class one day and Mr. Clarkson greeted him with a giant smile. The teacher told him he'd figured out how to tie shoes with one hand. He turned on a projector slide to keep the rest of the class busy and then took the young Abbott outside with two chairs and showed him his technique. It may seem like a small event, but it stuck with Jim Abbott for the rest of his life. It proved to be a lasting example that, no matter what he was born without, there would always be ways to overcome the challenges.

This lesson would be invaluable throughout the early years of Abbott's baseball career, especially when doubters and naysayers would tell him that playing in the major leagues wasn't possible for someone like him. Even when he was the best player on the team, most people couldn't look past him having only one hand.

No matter what criticism he faced, Abbott continued to pitch beyond any expectations, except his own. He always knew he was great.

Reaching The Bigs

Abbott would continue hearing doubters and so-called "harsh realities" until the end of his high school career. The Toronto Blue Jays selected him in the 1985 MLB draft. They even offered him a $50,000 bonus. The problem was the Blue Jays selected him in the final round of the draft. Rather than immediately pursue his dreams in the pros, Abbott opted to go to college instead. It was a wise decision that later proved to be the best choice.

A native of Flint, Michigan, Abbott went to the nearby Michigan University. During his time in college (1985–1988), his baseball accolades and achievements started to pile up. He was finally receiving the recognition his playing talents deserved.

In 1987, his sophomore year at Michigan University, Abbott and the Wolverines reached first place in the Big Ten Eastern Division. They'd go on to win the conference championship for the second year in a row. With an 11-3 record (and pitching a no-hitter in the NCAA tournament), Abbott was a significant part of the team's success. He would end up winning the Golden Spikes Award for his incredible season. Abbott became a global athlete the same year, participating in the Pan American Games. He even represented the country in the opening ceremonies. Team USA would win a silver medal in baseball.

For his achievements in college and the Pan American Games, the pitcher won the James E. Sullivan Award, given annually to an "outstanding" college-level or Olympic athlete. It is not just a performance-based award but also takes into account leadership, character, sportsmanship, and other qualities. He was the first baseball player to win the award.

A similar year of success occurred for Abbott in 1988. While the Wolverines wouldn't win the conference championship for another consecutive year, the one-handed pitcher had a terrific season. In fact, he was voted Big Ten Conference Player of the Year. It was another reward never given to a baseball player before. When the college season was over, Abbott went global again, competing in the 1988 Olympic Games in Seoul, South Korea. Abbott helped Team USA win gold medal honors, throwing a complete game in the final match against Team Japan.

With awards and successes accumulating, not to mention international recognition, it was time for Abbott to make the next step in his baseball career. He would opt out of his last year of college and enter the professional baseball scene.

Keep in mind, Abbott was selected in the last round by the Toronto Blue Jays the first time he was in the MLB draft, just three years earlier. When his name hit the 1988 draft list, the California Angels didn't waste much time drafting him. He was taken in the first round, eighth overall, and received a signing bonus four times the amount Toronto had offered in 1985. This showed exactly how the Angels felt about the pitcher with only one hand. Jim Abbott was a premier talent worthy of being a starting pitcher in the MLB.

"I Didn't Want To Be Like Pete Gray"

When drafted by a team in the majors, most players spent at least a season or two in the minor leagues. Even top draft picks need some time to mature and work on certain skills to be ready for the big time. Only a few rare players move seamlessly from the draft to the majors with no minor-league experience. Jim Abbott was one of those exceptions. He never played a single minor league game, becoming the 15th player since 1965, when the draft was implemented, to make his professional debut in the majors.

This was not the initial expectation. After being selected in the 1988 draft, Abbott reported to Spring Training. The assumption was that he would get some practice against pro-level hitters, before being sent to a minor league farm team. He changed these perceptions with his performance that spring, earning a spot in the starting rotation.

After his first Spring Training game, he answered media questions, explaining how he was able to pitch and field with only one hand. "I've been doing this since I was five. Now it's as natural as tying my shoes," he said, giving a small nod to his childhood experience with Mr. Clarkson.

When the season began, the world watched Abbott pitch his first professional baseball game. It was a widely televised event because of the media storm that his story generated. There were even television crews from other countries. His team lost, and Abbott only pitched a few innings. However, he received a standing ovation when he left the mound.

His third start, against the Baltimore Orioles, would be his first win. Putting the pressure of that first win behind him, Abbott pitched decently well the rest of the year. He had a 12-12 record with a 3.92 ERA. He was in the running for the American League Rookie of the Year honors, coming fifth in the voting.

The 1991 season was Abbott's most impressive one. His record was 18-11 and he ended with a 2.89 ERA. He almost won the Cy Young Award for being the best pitcher in the league. The following season his record slipped (7-15), but he improved his ERA to 2.77.

Abbott was traded to the New York Yankees in 1993. While his numbers began to slip during his time with the Yankees, he did manage an incredible feat. He pitched a no-hitter on September 4 against the Cleveland Indians. It was an incredible accomplishment for any pitcher, let alone a player with only one hand. It was the crowning experience of his MLB career and solidified him in baseball's history books as a legend.

The rest of Abbott's career wasn't so stellar. He had his worse year in 1996, pitching to a lowly record of 2-18. He retired from baseball for the 1997 season but would play part of 1998 and 1999. He had moments of glory that made it seem like he was coming back to his prime, but his performance began to falter again. He would retire permanently in 1999.

Throughout his career, Abbott received many comparisons to Pete Gray, but he did his best to change this narrative. "I wanted to be like Nolan Ryan. I didn't want to be like Pete Gray…I don't want kids to be like me because I have one hand. I want kids to be like Jim Abbott because he's a baseball pitcher."

While Abbott admitted his career had plenty of low points and that he was not destined for the Hall of Fame, he never blamed his disability. "I'll always be looked at as having played with one hand. How other people see it is up to them…The only thing that matters to me is a sense of giving everything I've got and making the most of what I've been given."

Jim Abbott approached baseball with this mentality. He gave it everything he had. He was an elite pitcher. He threw a no-hitter. His physical handicap was only a footnote in an incredible career. That's how baseball history should remember Jim Abbott's time in the MLB.

CHAPTER 2:

ICHIRO SUZUKI BRIDGES JAPANESE AND AMERICAN BASEBALL

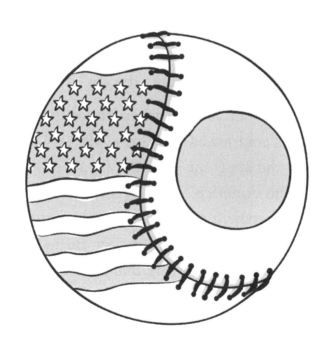

Japan loves baseball almost as much as America, possibly even more. The emphasis that we put on college football, the Japanese place on their college baseball teams. For decades, however, the baseball worlds of these two countries were kept separate.

Aside from Masanori Murakami, Major League Baseball had not seen Japanese talent except in exhibition games. Murakami's playing career created a rift between the Japanese and American baseball cultures that was not quickly repaired. While Japanese players revered baseball in America as the highest echelon of the sport, stiff contracts and their cultural guidelines kept players from making the jump across the Pacific to play in the US.

This all changed in 1995. Pitcher Hideo Nomo found a loophole in his contract as a Japanese player. By voluntarily retiring from the sport (at least, the Japanese side), he was free to move to America and play in the MLB. The move shocked Japan where newspapers were quick to label Nomo as a "traitor." His own father turned on him for betraying the country. Ignoring this negativity and shame, Nomo signed with the Los Angeles Dodgers.

As Nomo's MLB career gained momentum, the Japanese people changed their attitude. Suddenly, they revered their star overseas for showing the American people the quality of Japan's athletes. *Nomomania*, as it was known, swept from LA to Japan. Attendance at Dodger Stadium spiked whenever Nomo was pitching due to the groups of Japanese spectators. The stadium even opened a Japanese restaurant to satisfy the new patronage.

In Japan, every inning Nomo pitched was broadcasted across the country. Newspapers included his latest numbers and anything else worthy of reporting about the pitcher's MLB career. Nomo's actions opened the doors for future Japanese stars to make the jump to the MLB.

One of these players was Ichiro Suzuki. While Nomo opened the door, Ichiro tore the walls down between two baseball communities.

The Education Of Ichiro

Ichiro Suzuki showed promise and passion for baseball at a young age. His father, Nobuyuki Ichiro, encouraged his son's baseball dreams, committing himself to them as well. He would leave work early every day to help his son practice, no matter the weather. The father's dedication to his son's baseball skills bordered on cruelty.

One day, Ichiro was tired from practice and wanted to run off with his friends. When Nobuyuki denied him permission, the boy sat in the middle of the field and refused to move. The father began to throw balls at the protesting son. Luckily, Ichiro's knife-sharp reflexes allowed him to shift his body to avoid being hit.

The father-son team became frequent customers at the local batting cage. Ichiro, sometimes visiting the cages four times a day, would swing his bat hundreds to thousands of times. When he was 12, Ichiro wrote an essay about his career goals and hopes. It reflected both his determination to achieve his goals and the rigorous impact of his father's pressure to help the youngster succeed:

> *"My dream when I grow up is to be a first-class professional baseball player. I have the confidence to do the necessary practice to reach that goal. I started practicing from age three. From the age of nine, I have practiced baseball 360 out of 365 days a year and I practice hard. I only have five to six hours a year to play with my friends. That's how much I practiced. So, I think I can surely become a pro."*

Nobuyuki also instilled in his son many of the core philosophies and principles that would serve the player throughout his career. For example, Ichiro never showed emotion on the field. While other young players would jump up and down or cheer after a game, Ichiro did not. Nor would he slam his equipment around after a bad game or an embarrassing strikeout.

Ichiro rarely struck out at all. During a three-year high school career, he struck out only ten times over 536 at-bats. It was always a called strike; he never got out by swinging and missing the ball. In fact, when he swung, he made contact 97% of the time. His concentration at the plate was near-perfect.

The Will Of Ichiro

The education of Ichiro was not just the product of an over-aggressive parent determined to mold his son into an athlete through trial by father. Nobukyi's approach to Ichiro's training and education was attuned to what was normal in Japanese culture. Many of Japan's greatest coaches put players through military-like training. The belief was that players needed to know hardship and suffering to reach their full potential. This came from the samurai way of *bushido*. One has to suffer to be good.

After Ichiro left high school, he was drafted by the Orix BlueWave of the Pacific League in Japan. Scouts didn't like his lithe frame. Ichiro was 5'9" and weighed only 120 pounds. Thus, many disregarded his high school stats because he didn't "look" like a professional baseball player.

If this upset Ichiro, he never showed it. He would flourish in the Japanese minor leagues, leading with a .366 average. He even played games at the pro level, batting .253 in 40 games. The team manager, Shozo Doi, then made a bizarre decision to send the young player back to the minor leagues. He reasoned that Ichiro had come up too quickly and without any trouble. Doi believed Ichiro needed to know hardship before he was ready for the big leagues.

Again, Ichiro didn't reveal any discontent about the decision. Instead, he practiced harder and longer. This is saying something because Japanese baseball players already train at a level approaching lunacy. His only act of defiance was when Doi tried to change his swing. His swing was unconventional and something he and his father had worked on from a young age. Noboyuki had begged every coach in Ichiro's career not to mess with it.

Its oddness was tactical. Ichiro swung as a lefty, even though he was naturally right-handed. This was to put him closer to first base. When he swung, he turned his body in such a way that he was already pointed down the first base line. Paired with his speed, this allowed him to beat out infield hits with ease.

Out of politeness, Ichiro tried a more standard swing to please the manager. It sunk his average to the basement and prompted him to declare that he'd rather stay on the farm team than change the swing he'd been using since childhood. Doi sent him to the minor leagues, unwilling to put up with the player's stubbornness.

Luckily for Ichiro, Doi's time as team manager came to an end soon after. The new manager, Akira Ogi, was much more lenient. He saw Ichiro's incredible talent and quickly moved him to the lead-off spot in the BlueWave's starting lineup. Ichiro thanked Ogi by putting up legendary numbers that year. He became the first player in Japan to have over 200 hits in a season and ended the season with a .385 batting average.

A few years later, Ogi would come to Ichiro's rescue again. By this point, Ichiro was a household name in Japan. He was a sports rockstar. Yet, he began feeling like a big fish in a small pond. He dreamed of playing in America and putting his skills against the best players in the world.

While he could have taken the same route as Nomo to achieve this goal, Ichiro was more traditional. He believed he had an obligation and a duty to play for the BlueWave until he was no longer needed. That was the honorable thing to do.

Ogi recognized this and realized what he must do. He wanted Ichiro to stay, but he knew it was selfish. He released his star player from any obligations to the team. In the fall of 2000, Ichiro inked a deal with the Seattle Mariners. He was on his way to America.

The Impact Of Ichiro

Tensions between Japan and the US were ever-present in the 90s. It was a time when the Japanese auto industry was booming and threatening to usurp US companies like Ford, Chevy, and GMC. Japan was also creating electronic products largely considered to be superior to US brands. Yet, many Americans still held on to the belief that anything (or anyone) made in Japan was of poor quality.

This nationalistic pride leaked into baseball. After all, baseball was the American Pastime. Americans invented the sport. There was no way a small Japanese man could ever thrive in the big leagues. Japanese baseball was thought to be second-rate because of how they approached the game, especially their style of hitting.

Thus, there weren't many positive perceptions when Ichiro arrived at the Mariners' Spring Training. Even though Ichiro had put on about 20 pounds of muscle before arriving, critics still saw a thin man, especially compared to the hulking MLB sluggers of the era.

Lou Piniella, Ichiro's new manager in Seattle, thought it was unlikely Ichiro would be in the lineup on Opening Day. Piniella believed when Ichiro faced the pitchers in the US, they would cut him down to size, and the player from Japan was already small to start.

It didn't take long for Ichiro to prove his many critics wrong. He batted .321 through Spring Training and earned a spot on the starting roster. He quickly recorded his first two MLB hits during Mariners Opening Day. The second hit, a perfect bunt single in the ninth inning, sparked a come-from-behind win for Seattle.

By the start of June, Ichiro was a household name in American baseball, just as it was in his home country. He was on the cover of Sports Illustrated and leading the American League with a .366 batting average. Lou Piniella happily retracted any criticism he had of Ichiro. MLB pitchers couldn't figure out how to get him out. He could hit everything, evident by his swing-and-miss rate of only 6%.

It was clear it was not Ichiro that had to adapt to American baseball. American baseball had to adapt to Ichiro.

By the end of his first year with the Mariners, he had a mile-long list of accolades and records. In total, he broke 13 MLB, American League, or team records. He became the second player in history to win both the AL MVP and Rookie of the Year awards, leading the league in most of the offensive stat categories. Defensively, he won a Gold Glove.

Contrary to initial perceptions, American audiences loved Ichiro's style of hitting. It was an ode to baseball's past when players didn't swing for the fences. They swung to get on base. Ichiro's hitting at the top of the Mariners' lineup was an offensive spark. The team would routinely score a run in the first inning, even before their power hitters, like Ken Griffey Jr. and Alex Rodriguez, came to bat.

The Achievement Of Ichiro

Everyone wanted to get inside the mind of Ichiro. His muted expression on the field and Zen-like persona only encouraged the media to try harder to crack his shell. It never worked. When asked what his objectives were in baseball, he simply replied, "I'm working toward my own inner goals." He would not elaborate any further.

He was even more muted about his own achievements and successes. "I really don't like the word success or a lot of talk about records," he said as part of a documentary on his historic first season. "I don't mean to say they have no value or are insignificant, but the most important thing is doing your best, preparing, giving your all. If you get a record without preparation, it's not satisfying. If you really prepare, try hard, do your best, and you succeed in surpassing yourself, that is really satisfying...So instead of thinking about who is number one and who is number two, you should think about whether you have given your best."

It's this level of wisdom that Ichiro would often keep to himself, adding to his mystique as baseball's most inscrutable player. Whenever he did decide to dispense his thoughts, it was immediately apparent how wise a player he was.

Later in his career, he shared a glimpse of what he viewed as his most significant accomplishment during his time playing in the US. "I think I have narrowed the gap between America and Japan," Ichiro said. As always, he was correct. *Ichiromania* swept across Japan and the US, bringing the two cultures together in profound ways.

In Seattle, there was an economic boom. Travel agencies sold Ichiro baseball packages to Japanese tourists, boosting hotel and airline reservations dramatically and dumping millions of dollars into the city's economy. Pacific Northwesterners were quick to pick up Japanese words of encouragement from the international tourists they now shared the stands with during games. They also developed a love for sushi, especially the *Ichirolls* sold at Safeco Field. Signage at the stadium and even across downtown Seattle bore Japanese kanji characters. *Ichiromania* caused Seattle to become multicultural in just one baseball season and without anyone having to leave the city limits.

Across the Pacific Ocean, in Japan, a similar *Ichiromania was* sweeping the nation. Japan used to sporadically watch US baseball, mainly when a pitcher like Hideo Nomo was playing. Now, they had a player in the everyday lineup to root for. Even with the 16-hour time difference, Japanese audiences consumed Mariners baseball with a religious-like devotion. The first question at the water cooler in the morning was, "How did Ichiro do?"

The real sensationalism of Ichiro in Japan stemmed from how he was received in America. In the postwar era, there was always unease between the cultures. Nonetheless, Ichiro was revered by both audiences. It inspired the Japanese and thrilled the Americans to see the slender Ichiro playing among the musclemen of the MLB. They almost couldn't believe that a Japanese player was so idolized by US audiences.

Just by playing baseball his way, swinging the bat how he liked, Ichiro showed Americans how talented Japanese athletes were. In turn, this restored pride in Japan and changed the perception of their players playing in the US. It was once thought of as a shame to choose to play in the US over Japan. Now, it was an honor.

Ichiro showed that the power of baseball can extend beyond a country's borders. One man inspired two nations to mix cultures and enjoy a sport together.

CHAPTER 3:

THE BOSTON RED SOX REVERSE THE CURSE

No sport carries more superstitions than baseball. Ask any player and they'll tell you about a ritual or good luck charm they swear is vital to their success. It may be a song they listen to before the game, a special pair of socks, or a home-run-inducing dance. The most well-known baseball superstitions come in the form of curses. And one of the most prolific of these hexes was The Curse of the Bambino, which plagued the Boston Red Sox and their fans for 86 years.

The namesake of this curse comes from the legendary baseball player Babe Ruth. One of his many nicknames was The Great Bambino. (He also went by other monikers, like the Sultan of Swat and the Behemoth of Bust, just to name a few).

Ruth himself did not utter any curse against the Red Sox team. He was actually a member of the Red Sox and helped the team earn three championships between 1915 and 1918 before he was traded to the New York Yankees. In fact, the name of the curse wasn't commonly used prior to Dan Shaughnessy's 1990 book *The Curse of the Bambino.*

Ruth's trading to the New York Yankees marked a notable decline in the Red Sox. They went from being the most winning team to not achieving World Series glory for 86 years.

In 2004, the Red Sox had a chance to end the curse once and for all. The only problem was they trailed their arch-rivals, the New York Yankees, 0-3 in a best-of-seven ALCS. They needed to win four straight games to overcome the deficit and make it to the World Series, a feat that had never been done before in the sport of baseball.

Baseball's Biggest Losers For 86 Years

The 86-year World Series drought of the Red Sox is a history of losing in some of the most catastrophic ways imaginable. It wasn't so much the losses that led to claims of the Red Sox being cursed. It was *how* they would lose. They elevated it to an art form.

In 1975, with an early 3-0 lead, the Red Sox lost in the ninth inning of Game Seven of the World Series against the Reds. Three years later, Bucky Dent of the New York Yankees hit a ball that kissed the top of Boston's Green Monster for a home run. A centimeter lower and the ball stays in the park.

Columnist George Vecsey officially labeled the team cursed after their loss to the New York Mets in the 1986 World Series. The Red Sox were leading the series 3-2 in Game Six. Things seemed to be going well. The Red Sox had a lead in the tenth inning and only needed to hold the Mets. Then, the Curse of the Bambino struck one of its most devastating chords yet.

First, the Mets would score the tying run on a wild pitch from Bob Stanley. Next, Mookie Wilson would hit a weak grounder to first base. Red Sox first baseman Bill Buckner had fielded thousands of balls just like this one throughout his life. It should have been an easy play, almost automatic. Yet, the ball rolled between his legs and the Mets scored the winning run.

In the following game, the Mets would win the World Series with a score of 8-5. It was one of the most devastating failures of a team in World Series history. Even the biggest doubters of curses and hocus pocus started to believe that this thing was real.

The year 2003 marked another chapter for Boston's losing history in baseball. It was Game Seven of the ALCS and Boston faced the New York Yankees. With a 5-2 lead in the eighth inning, things seemed promising once again for Red Sox Nation. In an unorthodox decision, Red Sox manager Grady Little kept Pedro Martínez, the starting pitcher, in the game. He didn't opt to go to the bullpen, which was the more conventional move. His decision allowed the New York Yankees to rally against the exhausted pitcher, scoring three runs on four hits and forcing extra innings.

The Yankees would seal the fate of the cursed Boston Red Sox with a walk-off home run in the 11th inning by Aaron Boone. Grady Little's poor decision-making became heavily criticized after the loss and ultimately cost him his job.

A year later, the Red Sox found themselves in familiar territory. They were back in the ALCS facing the New York

Yankees once more. While fans and players alike were hopeful that this was the *Reverse the Curse* year, things quickly went from bad to worse. The Yankees won the first three games of the series. The Red Sox would need to win all of the remaining for games to secure a spot in the World Series.

Game Four: The Dave Roberts Steal

Only a night earlier, the crowd at Fenway watched their hated rivals score a crushing 19 runs to win Game Three. One Sox fan held a sign that read, "I can't believe we fell for it again." The substantial defeat would have been the last nail in the coffin for most teams.

For most of Red Sox Nation, the hope was just to avoid the humiliation of being swept away. After all, beating the Yankees once is a daunting enough task. Trying to beat them four times in a row, especially in the postseason, felt like an impossibility. Yet, the Red Sox players seemed in oddly high spirits while warming up for Game Four.

Before the start of the game, Red Sox first baseman Kevin Millar said, "It happens. This is baseball," in reference to the colossal loss the night before. "But let me tell you," he continued, "don't let us win today. We got [Pedro] tomorrow, [Schilling] in Game Six. Then, Game Seven, anything can happen. This is it. Do not let the Sox win this game."

The Yankees seemed more than happy to comply. While the Yankees didn't score in the first inning, something they'd done in every previous game of the series, they did strike first. Derek Jeter got on base in the third inning before Alex Rodriguez lifted a two-run home run over Fenway's Green Monster.

To make matters worse for those still holding hope in Boston, the Yankees' starting pitcher, Orlando Hernández, was leaving Red Sox batters mystified. Through four innings, he allowed only one hit and two walks, hardly enough offense to mount the incredible comeback Boston needed.

Eventually, Hernández would start to lose steam. He found himself in hot water in the fifth inning after walking two batters. He almost escaped trouble, but Orlando Cabrera had other plans. He started a fifth inning, two-out rally with a single that scored Bill Mueller. After another walk, David Ortiz swatted a ball into centerfield that put two more runs on the scoreboard: 3-2 Boston. It was only the second time in the series that Boston held a lead.

Any jubilation that Red Sox Nation felt was quickly eliminated. New York responded in the next half-inning. Hideki "Godzilla" Matsui put an end to Red Sox starter Derek Lowe's night, bringing Mike Timlin in relief.

The events over the next few batters invoked emotions familiar to the Boston Red Sox's identity as baseball history's biggest losers. Three of the next four Yankees batters reached base on infield singles. The Boston infield seemed determined to kick, bobble, and drop the ball as much as possible.

Had it not been for Bernie Williams getting caught stealing, the Yankees may have put Game Four to rest and kept the Curse of the Bambino alive. Luckily, the Red Sox avoided an utter fiasco and escaped the inning down by only one run. Ironically, Boston got out of the inning on an infield grounder with the bases loaded.

The Red Sox couldn't answer back in the bottom of the sixth inning, nor the seventh or eighth. With only three outs left, their time was running short. The only solace was it was still a one-run game. There was still some hope left for Red Sox Nation.

In came the Yankees' ineffable closer, Mariano Rivera. Throughout his career (1995–2013), Rivera blew only 80 saves in 732 regular-season opportunities. In other words, Rivera got the job done nine out of ten times. Remarkably, his postseason pitching was even better. He was 8-1 in postseason appearances and had a 0.69 ERA. When he entered the game, most opposing players saw it as a death sentence.

Luckily for Red Sox Nation, Kevin Millar was not of this school of thought. He battled for a lead-off walk. Red Sox manager Terry Francona quickly called upon Dave Roberts to pinch-run for the sluggish Millar. He gave Roberts a wink as he left the dugout to relieve Millar, as if to say, "Go do your thing."

A game of cat and mouse ensued once Roberts took Millar's place. Rivera threw over to first several times, hoping to catch the baserunner. He held the ball for what seemed like years. But Roberts was not shaken. He continued to take significant leads each time, drawing more throws over. Rivera knew Roberts was going to steal. *Everyone* knew Roberts was going to steal. And, on Rivera's first pitch to the plate, he did.

"The Steal," as it became known, marked the turning point of the entire series. Bill Mueller would hit a single up the middle, enabling the speedy Roberts to score and tie the game. The Red Sox had some life as the game headed into extra innings.

There were chances for both teams to score in the 11th, adding to the intensity of the game. However, it would ultimately be in the 12th inning when the game finally saw its end. David Ortiz hit a two-run home run to stun the home crowd and Yankee Stadium and force Game Five.

Game Five: David Ortiz Does It Again

Pedro Martínez had been with the Red Sox since 1998. It was the last year before his contract would end and he'd become a free agent. With elimination on the table for Boston, Game Five could have been the last time Red Sox Nation saw their beloved starter pitch for the home crowd at Fenway Park.

The players, on the other hand, were fighting tired muscles and frazzled nerves. The extra-inning affair of Game Four lasted over five hours and ended after midnight. This gave both teams only 16 hours to sleep, recover, and prepare for the start of Game Five. Ortiz said during warmups, "When I woke up this morning. I thought my shoulder was on the other side of the bed."

Soreness aside, Ortiz got the first RBI of the game with a single. Catcher Jason Varitek would walk with the bases loaded to notch a second run for Boston. In the next half an inning, the Yankees responded with a solo home run from Bernie Williams.

Aside from the Williams home run, the Red Sox ace ran into little trouble through the first five innings. He also managed to strike out seven Yankees batters. Offensively, Boston's bats did little to give their pitcher extra support and the game remained 2-1 into the sixth inning. This is where the trouble began for Pedro and the Red Sox.

The inning started smoothly, and Pedro got a quick first out. Then, Jorge Posada and Ruben Sierra got back-to-back singles for New York. With the pitch count rising and runners threatening to score, Pedro's composure was compromised. He hit Miguel Cairo with a pitch and loaded the bases for the Yankees' captain, Derek Jeter.

To appreciate the intensity of this pitcher-batter duel, you have to understand that Jeter was one of baseball's greatest postseason performers. He was also a tremendous clutch hitter, coming up big for the Yankees in crucial moments. Batting with the bases loaded in a decisive Game Five against the division rivals was the precise situation that Jeter thrived on the most.

True to his "Captain Clutch" nickname, Jeter delivered. He swung late on an outside pitch to shoot it down the first base line and into the corner. It was a bases-clearing double and suddenly the Yankees shot ahead 4-2. It also marked the end of Pedro's night and possibly his last pitching performance as a member of the Boston squad.

The Red Sox found themselves in a familiar situation - needing to mount a comeback to stay alive. Ortiz would spark some hope with a home run to start the bottom of the eighth inning, making the score 4-3 in favor of the Yankees.

The next few minutes of play were an eerie replay of the events of Game Four. Kevin Millar, representing the tying run, walks, and Dave Roberts comes in to pinch run. Mariano Rivera would even come in to pitch to complete the recreation. The result of the inning was also the same. Roberts managed to get himself around the bases and tie the game on a Trot Nixon single and Jason Varitek sacrifice fly.

Red Sox Nation caught a lucky break in the ninth inning. Tony Clark hit a ball to deep right with a runner on first. The ball dropped in front of the wall and bounced over for a ground-rule double. Had it stayed in the park, Ruben Sierra, the runner, would have scored and given the Yankees the lead. Instead, the ground-rule double meant he was forced to stop at third. The Red Sox would get out of that inning unscathed.

What came next was another extra-inning battle. While there were moments of drama and chances to score, the game remained 4-4 until the bottom of the 14th inning. With two runners on, Ortiz came to the plate once more. Less than 24 hours earlier he had ended Game Four with a walk-off home run. And he'd already scored twice in this game. He was the perfect candidate to preserve the Red Sox season once again.

The Yankees may have had Captain Clutch, but the Boston Red Sox had Big Papi. He hit a line-drive single to score a run and end the 14-inning saga, which was the longest postseason game on record at 5 hours and 49 minutes. The Red Sox had officially done what only two other teams managed: force a Game Six after being down 0-3. Could they be the first to win Game Six and, better yet, Game Seven?

Game Six: Schilling's Bloody Sock

In a book about inspirational baseball stories, an entire chapter could be spent detailing Curt Schilling's efforts on the mound in Game Six of the 2004 ALCS and his famous bloody sock.

Schilling was a new acquisition by the Boston Red Sox. Shortly after the trade, he appeared as a hitchhiker in a commercial for the Ford F-150. When the Ford truck stops to pick him up, the driver asks, "So, where ya headed?" Schilling responds, "Boston, gotta break an 86-year-old curse." Game Six was his opportunity to do just that, but there was one problem.

On October 5, during Game 1 of the ALDS versus the Angels, Schilling tore the peroneal tendon on his right ankle. "Every step made me question my ability to pitch," Schilling said. The injury was an apparent detriment in his first game against the Yankees. The Bronx Bombers shelled him for six runs in only three innings.

Ignoring injury and recent defeat, Schilling took the mound on Game Six. Before the game, Bill Morgan, the Red Sox team doctor, performed a small surgery on the ankle in the training room. Morgan stitched the skin of Schilling's ankle to the tissue around the tendon, hoping it would hold everything together. It was a barbaric, temporary fix, but it was enough for Schilling and the Red Sox to take the field.

Before he even reached the mound, Schilling's sock had a notable red stain. His ankle was bleeding. Nonetheless, Schilling pitched through the obvious discomfort, even as the stain grew larger each inning. It was all anyone could look at. Even the game's broadcast scarcely spent more than a few minutes without zooming in on the bloody spot.

In the ESPN 30-for-30 documentary *Four Days in October,* Schilling describes his thoughts on the mound:

> *I was more concerned with the fact that I couldn't really feel my shoe. My foot was bleeding and the blood was going to the bottom of my sock. It was so wet I could only feel half my foot. So, I kept trying to have to push my foot and adjust my foot to make sure my shoe was on tight.*

During and after the game, many people asked the question, "Why didn't the Yankees bunt?" Schilling had limited mobility. Bunting would force him off the mound and put more pressure on his wounded ankle. After the game, Yankees manager Joe Torre said he didn't want to change their game plan and didn't realize the severity of the injury.

At one point, a grounder to the first baseman required Schilling to dash to the bag and cover for the out. He made the play, but his walk back to the mound was slow and he had an obvious limp. Seeing this may have changed Joe Torre's mind about bunting, but Schilling's night was over shortly after.

Schilling pitched for seven innings and threw 98 pitches on his bad ankle. He allowed just one run on a Bernie Williams home run. The score was 4-1 in favor of Boston, largely thanks to a Mark Bellhorn three-run homer.

Bronson Arroyo came in for relief and promptly let up a run on a Derek Jeter single, making the score 4-2 and bringing Alex Rodriguez, the game-tying run, to the plate. The home crowd at Yankee Stadium began to get loud again.

Rodriguez hit a weak grounder down the first base line, which Arroyo fielded quickly. It seemed like an easy out, but the ball suddenly slipped from Arroyo's glove and rolled down the line. Rodriguez reached second and Derek Jeter scored. The play came under review.

Arroyo and the Red Sox argued that A-Rod had slapped the ball from the glove, thereby interfering with the play. Replay showed Rodriguez making clear contact with Arroyo's glove using his hand. While the Yankees slugger tried to argue that it was his running motion and not an intentional interference, the umpires disagreed. Rodriguez was called out for interference. Jeter had to return to first base.

With all of the drama surrounding Schilling's bloody sock, you would think that this game couldn't get any wilder, but this was the Yankees and the Red Sox rivalry. Upset by the overturned call, Yankees fans began throwing debris onto the field. The situation grew so intense that the Red Sox players left the field for their own safety. Later on, NYPD officers in protective riot gear would line the third and first base lines near the stands, hoping to deter the unruly home crowd from causing any more disturbances.

Boston closer Keith Foulke came out to pitch in the bottom of the ninth inning. It was his third relief appearance in three days. With one out remaining, Tony Clark came to bat with two runners on. The score was still 4-2, meaning Clark had the opportunity to win the game on a home run and crush the hopes of Red Sox Nation. Foulke had other plans. He got Clark out on a swinging strike.

The 2004 Boston Red Sox officially became the first team to force a Game Seven after an 0-3 deficit. While it was an incredible feat, everyone focused on Schilling and his pitching performance.

"His heart is so big...I guarantee you he didn't feel that good, but he competed and pitched his butt off," said Francona in the post-game interview. Millar also weighed in on Schilling's performance in *Four Days in October.* "What he did that day was heroic - bottom line. This guy had surgery on a tendon in his ankle and was able to throw in probably the biggest game of his life."

It was time for the final chapter, for better or for worse.

Game Seven: The Curse Is Lifted

Kevin Millar's words before Game Four were ringing in the ears of Red Sox fans everywhere. "Game Seven, anything can happen." Yet, some people still felt that the Curse of the Bambino would strike once again. Yankees fans saw it as a game they couldn't lose. The team had never lost a Game Seven at home. They just had to wait for the cursed Red Sox to make the catastrophic mistakes they were known for.

"I know how this ends, because I've been watching it all my life," said one Red Sox fan and true believer of the Curse. Yet, another thought resonated in the minds of Boston hopefuls. Maybe this - winning four straight against the Yankees - is how the curse is supposed to end? This is the way to exorcise this thing once and for all!

The game would start off rocky for the Red Sox when Damon was thrown out at home trying to score. The lump in the throats of Red Sox Nation suddenly grew. The negative feelings didn't last long. The enduring hero of the team, David Ortiz quickly clubbed a home run and gave the Sox an early 2-0 lead.

In the second inning, Johnny Damon really broke the score open with a grand slam: 6-0 Red Sox. In any other circumstance, this early lead would feel great. When it comes to playing the New York Yankees, no one is comfortable with a 6-0 lead, especially not in the postseason. Worse yet, this was the Red Sox. They had a history of falling apart and blowing leads in crucial games.

Later in the game, Damon would strike again for another home run and push the score to 8-1. To make matters worse for the Bronx Bombers, Derek Lowe, on two days of rest, was pitching a gem for Boston. He had allowed only one hit through six innings. The Yankees suddenly were short on time. The home crowd at Yankee Stadium had a dejected look that Red Sox Nation knew all too well.

Life sparked back into the home crowd when the Red Sox brought Pedro Martínez in to pitch. Pedro Martínez had a history of troublesome outings against the Yankees. After a particularly poor pitching performance, Martínez said in a post-game interview, "What can I say but tip my hat and call the Yankees my daddy." New York fans obliged. As Pedro took the mound, the crowd began chanting, "Who's your daddy?" It was all anyone could hear.

While Martínez did let up a couple of runs, the 8-1 lead proved to be enough of a cushion for him. With the score 10-3, Alan Embree pitched to Rubén Sierra with runners on first and second. Sierra hit a grounder to Sox second baseman Pokey Reese, who threw to first and solidified the improbable comeback.

The 2004 Boston Red Sox had done what many believed was impossible. They overcame a 3-0 deficit against the New York Yankees and won in Game Seven. They were headed to the World Series. Only seven days later, they would finish a sweep of the St. Louis Cardinals and become champions, shattering their 86-year drought and putting to rest, once and for all, the Curse of the Bambino.

This story isn't inspirational because of the comeback. It's not because of Schilling's blood sock, the David Ortiz walk-offs, or Dave Roberts' steal. It isn't inspirational because it broke a curse and led to the first World Series win for Boston in 86 years.

The 2004 Boston Red Sox are inspirational because they believed more than anyone, even the fans, that they were the team to do this. They believed before they even won Game Four. They believed in themselves against insurmountable odds and obstacles.

CHAPTER 4:

THE MIAMI MARLINS AND THE COVID-19 BASEBALL SEASON

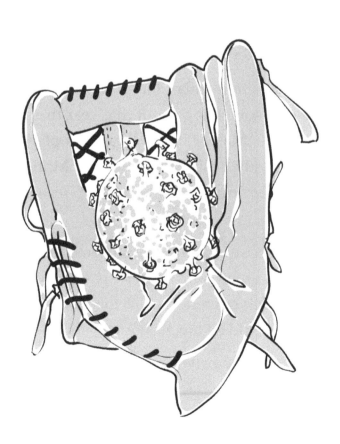

The 2019 Miami Marlins finished a whopping 40 games behind first place, carrying a losing record of 57 wins and 105 losses. They were the third-worst team in Major League Baseball and managed a lowly .352 winning percentage. Through 2021 and 2022, the team improved only slightly to scratch a .426 winning percentage.

These stats shouldn't scream "playoff-caliber team" to anyone. Yet, in the 2020 season, the Marlins were just that. They finished four games out of first place in the NL East and managed a .517 win percentage.

While you may not remember the 2020 Marlins being in the playoffs, there is something about that year that no one can forget: COVID-19. Major League Baseball's plans for a full season were quickly dashed. Initially, the MLB postponed the remained of Spring Training, hoping to resume play at a safer time.

The decision to postpone the season came at a time when the world didn't know how long the pandemic would last. It quickly became apparent that, if there was to be a 2020 season at all, it would be much shorter.

This sparked a debate between the league and the players' association about what exactly that season would look like. Ultimately, the two agreed on an abbreviated season consisting of 60 games. Teams would primarily play divisional opponents to restrict travel, thereby limiting chances for possible exposure. Then, there would be an expanded playoff tournament to decide the World Series champions.

Many detractors of the success of the Marlins in 2020 state that it was the 60-game season and expanded postseason that made their playoff berth possible. In a typical, 162-game season, their performance would have waned. In other words, these critics felt that their performance was more a matter of a lucky streak than a good baseball team.

There is some legitimacy behind this claim. Analysts put the 2020 Marlins' playoff chances at 0.2% in the normal season length with ten teams in the playoff. With the season revised to 60 games and 16 teams in the playoffs, their odds jumped to 9.2% to make the playoffs.

This terrible, life-threatening virus gave the Marlins a silver lining. However, it quickly turned on Miami Marlins.

An Unplanned Rebuilding

The first series of 2020 for the Marlins was against the Phillies. They won two out of three games. Before the start of the third game, Marlins pitcher José Ureña tested positive for COVID-19. Under the direction of the MLB, the teams went ahead and played the final game, but it proved to be a fatal misstep.

As more and more positive results appeared in the Marlins organization, including both players and coaching staff, their entire season came to a screeching halt. In total, 18 players tested positive, and two members of the coaching staff. It was almost the entire team. Many people expected it would be the end of the entire season. MLB commissioner Robert Manfred threatened a shutdown if players and teams didn't improve their behavior.

While the Marlins were allowed to continue their season, they needed to fill in the massive hole that COVID-19 put in their team. They would also need to replay several games they missed in the interim, which would be a tremendous challenge during the shortened season.

The bullpen was the first challenge. The coronavirus outbreak put eight relievers on the injured list, leaving only four healthy. In a flurry of moves, they grabbed ten new pitchers. First was a trade for James Hoty from Cleveland. Then another trade to grab an aging (but still effective) Richard Bleier from Baltimore. The Marlins would also sign two players named Josh Smith, plus Pet Venditte (known for being an ambidextrous pitcher), Nick Vincent, Brian Moran, Justin Shafer, Jorge Guzman, and Brett Eibner - a converted outfielder from an independent baseball team.

With the pitching staff covered, the next step was to fill in position players. The Marlins would find free agents Logan Forsythe (infielder), Wilkin Castillo (catcher), Eddie Alvarez (infielder), and others.

It was a busy few days for the Marlins, but they managed to reassemble a viable baseball team. The only question was whether it was competitive enough to win games. Moreover, was it a team that could *survive* the next 54 days where the Marlins would have to play 57 games to make up for the lost time? Another outbreak would put everything in jeopardy.

The Miami Bottom Feeders

In the first game of the 2020 season, the Marlins beat the Phillies 5-2. This prompted Ricky Bottalico, an NBC Sports analyst from Philadelphia, to make the statement, "you have to beat the bottom feeders. And, if you don't think the Marlins are bottom feeders, we'll see what happens in a couple weeks."

This comment came before any of the trouble with COVID-19 sidelining the majority of the Marlins' starting roster. It came after just one game of the season. The attitude of the Marlins players in response to the comment was simple: How can you call us bottom feeders after just one game of the season? Rather than lash back at Bottalico, the Marlins turned the bottom feeders' insult into their motivating mantra, even wearing shirts with the moniker proudly displayed.

Whatever their motivation was in the 2020 season, it seemed to work. Their replacement team managed to win seven games and lose eight before any of the COVID-positive players returned. When the regular squad began to trickle back, the Miami Marlins took off. Core players, such as Miguel Rojas and Brian Anderson, became offensive ignitors, driving the team to more and more wins.

When the trade deadline hit, the Marlins were, surprising to everyone, a buyer. They added the star power of outfielder Starling Marte. It was arguably the only known baseball name on the entire roster of Miami Bottom Feeders.

Phillies Versus Marlins Play Seven Games In Five Days

When the Marlins had to pause their season because of a COVID-19 outbreak, the Phillies were in the same boat. After the two teams played each other in the fatal first series of the season that lead to Miami's outbreak, Philadelphia also had to pause its season. The only difference was the Phillies had very few positive tests, especially compared to the 20 that the Marlins organization faced.

The catch-up schedules of both teams came to a head with a seven series between the two teams. This series was scheduled to be played over just five days, meaning there would be two doubleheaders in the mix.

During the first game of the series, the Marlins' latest acquisition, Starling Marte, faced off against the Phillies' newest player, Brandon Workman, in a bases-loaded situation. Marte won the battle with a double that cleared the bases, tying the game at 6-6. Jorge Alfaro would win the game with a walk-off hit in the bottom of the ninth inning.

The next day was a doubleheader that saw the Phillies trouncing the Marlins 12-0 in the first contest. Miami came back later that day and won 5-3. The next day saw the second Phillies win, bringing the series of seven to two games each. Then, the Marlins would win the next three games against their 2020 rivals, the team that inadvertently gave Miami their 'Bottom Feeders' nickname.

After this series, the Marlins went from a 35% chance to enter the playoffs to an 80% chance. It's worth reminding readers that, at the start of the shortened 2020 season, Miami only had a 9% chance to enter the postseason. A few days later, the Marlins officially punched their playoff ticket against the Cubs, putting to rest any thoughts about them being bottom feeders.

Brandon Kintzler, the closer of the Marlins, gave credit to the originator of the nickname. "I don't care if we're bottom feeders. I want to thank Ricky Bottalico for that motivation in opening weekend in Philadelphia by the way," said Kintzler. "He's probably the one that sent the Phillies home for that…You can't get rid of us."

Kintzler may have been riding a high from playing a decisive role in the playoff-clinching game for the Marlins.

Nonetheless, he was right. The Marlins were in the postseason.

The 2020 Marlins In The Playoffs

Statistically, the Marlins were not a playoff team. Not only did they have a negative run differential (263 runs scored versus 304 runs allowed), but the 2020 Miami team also posted poor league rankings across the board. Had the season been played to 162 games, it's unlikely that Miami would have come close to the playoffs.

But the 2020 season was not a typical season, and the Marlins were not a typical baseball team. Every game saw a radically different roster from the day before and featured a hodge-podge of replacements and starting players. This speaks to the mystery of Miami's success. It came down to the front office and their ability to plug and play throughout the season. It was also a testament to manager Don Mattingly's ability to coach every player to enter his clubhouse.

The other secret sauce of the Marlins was their ability to win doubleheader games. In a normal season, this is a rare event and features two nine-inning games. In the 2020 COVID-19 season, doubleheaders were only seven-inning affairs. The Marlins played *a lot* of doubleheaders - seven in total, for 14 total games, almost a quarter of the season.

Through all of these double features, the Marlins had a record of 10-4.

Whatever that you want to attribute the Marlins' success in 2020, they entered the postseason as the dark horse. Throughout baseball's history, the team had been in the playoffs two other times. They won the World Series on both occasions (1997 and 2003). This put a weird aura on their entrance into the 2020 postseason. Would they continue their undefeated playoff winning streak, or would the house of cards come tumbling down?

Fate would choose the latter, but not before the Marlins defeated the Chicago Cubs in the first round of the playoffs. This was no easy feat. The Cubs had won the World Series only four years prior and their team had star talents, like Javier Báez, Kris Bryant, Anthony Rizzo, Yu Darvish, and Craig Kimbrel. They even won their division in 2020. Yet, the bottom-feeding Marlins had little trouble. They won the series two games to nil.

Afterwards, they would fall to the Atlanta Braves in the NLDS. The Braves would actually sweep the Marlins, winning three straight. Regardless, any Marlins fan will tell you the season was a win in their minds. It was a team that went from being one of the worst in baseball to a playoff contender that made it all the way to the divisional series.

The 2020 Miami Marlins got further than anyone (aside from maybe themselves) thought they would. They overcame a

COVID-19 outbreak that sidelined almost their entire roster and still managed to outplay many of the year's top teams. Don Mattingly would win the award for manager of the year after continuously putting a highly competitive team on the field each day and working with a revolving door of new and old players.

Critics of the Marlins in 2020 cite many reasons why the team wasn't a "true" playoff contender. That said, you can't argue with their record and tenacity throughout the season. The real reason the 2020 Marlins have critics and detractors is that no one thought they'd be here at all. They were bottom feeders. Yet, their bottom-feeder mentality was exactly why they won.

The bottom line: you decide who you are - not the critics. You can either believe what they say about you or rise to the occasion and prove them wrong.

CHAPTER 5:

THE SEARCH FOR THE SHOT HEARD 'ROUND THE WORLD

Anyone who has ever held a baseball bat has, at one time or another, envisioned themselves at the plate, with the season on the line, hitting a home run to win it all for their team. Baseball's history books are full of walk-off heroics and iconic game-winning home runs like this. But there was a time when such incredible events were just fairy tales - until Bobby Thomson came along.

> *"Now it is done. Now the story ends. And there is no way to tell it. The art of fiction is dead. Reality has strangled invention. Only the utterly impossible, the inexpressibly fantastic, can ever be plausible again."*

These are the words of Red Smith describing what's become known in baseball as "The Shot Heard 'Round the World" or "The Miracle of Coogan's Bluff." Bobby Thomson of the New York Giants hit a game-winning home run in the bottom of the ninth inning during a must-win contest to clinch the National League Pennant from the cross-town rival (and favorites to win) Brooklyn Dodgers.

It was the most significant home run in baseball history at the time. Many people argue that it still is. With one swing of his bat, Thomson brought to life every fan's imagination. Artifacts from the game, like Thomson's bat and shoes, have been enshrined in the Baseball Hall of Fame and Museum. One piece of the historic event - the ball - has never been found.

The Giants And Dodgers Rivalry

Modern baseball fans know the rivalry between the San Francisco Giants and Los Angeles Dodgers. Some may be surprised to learn that this feud has been going on long before Major League Baseball ever moved to the West Coast.

The six- to seven-hour drive (more with traffic) between these two teams was once just a short subway ride across New York City. The Dodgers played in Brooklyn while the Giants resided in Manhattan. Then, both teams moved to their new homes in California. In fact, Dodgers owner Walter O'Malley suggested to Giants ownership to move the team to San Francisco to keep the rivalry alive.

It wasn't just geographical proximity that kept the contests between these teams exciting. The Brooklyn Dodgers' fanbase was blue-collar and represented the working class of New York. Conversely, fans of the New York Giants were primarily upper class and "gentlemen". These differences provided great fodder for both sides throughout the early years of the rivalry.

Adding more fuel to the fire were several personal feuds between members of each club. For example, Charles Ebbets, the owner of the Dodgers, had a long-standing hatred for Giants manager John McGraw. These emotions spread to nearly every player on these teams and the fans who loved to watch them play.

Jack Biegel was one of the millions of people inhabiting New York City during the height of the Dodgers and Giants rivalry. He grew up in the shadow of Ebbets Field, where the Dodgers played, giving him little choice regarding which New York fanbase he'd join.

Biegel had baseball aspirations of his own. He'd play amateur ball in Kentucky for a bit, hoping it'd be a steppingstone to one day play for his Brooklyn Dodgers. While he played well, he missed Brooklyn and couldn't handle the taunting from fans. He moved home and found himself in Manhattan at a job interview on October 3, 1951.

The date would stick in Biegel's mind for decades, but not because this new job would change his life. October 3, 1951 was the date that broke the hearts of Dodgers fans everywhere. A short distance from where Biegel was interviewing, at the Polo Grounds, Bobby Thomson was making history.

To understand the significance of the October home run, you have to go back to mid-August. The Brooklyn Dodgers had a substantial lead on the only contending teams - the New York Giants and the Philadelphia Phillies. It seemed certain that they would face the Yankees in the World Series.

The Giants had other plans. Coming down the last stretch of the season, they won 16 straight games and used this momentum to slingshot themselves within striking distance of their rivals. The Dodgers did little to prevent the comeback. While the Giants were busy winning all of their remaining seven games, the Brooklyn team kept losing. The season ended with the Dodgers and Giants both at 96-58 records. To break the tie, the teams would play a three-game series. The NY rivals split the first two games, leaving October 3 as the decisive match to determine who would go to the World Series.

The rest of the story is baseball legend. Bobby Thomson hits a home run off Dodgers' Ralph Branca in the ninth inning and sends the Giants to the playoffs. It's an inspiring story, but not the one you're about to read. This is the story of what happened after the ball disappeared into the stands.

The Spark That Started A Search And A Passion

Jack Biegel was older now and browsing a Salvation Army store where he came across a vintage-looking baseball. It had the yellowed tint of time. As his fingers turned the aged ball over, he noticed some familiar signatures: Willie Mays, Leo Durocher, Sal Maglie, Larry Jansen, Bobby Thomson, and almost every other member of the Giants 1951 team.

Even though he supported the Dodgers, Biegel paid a few dollars for the ball. After all, these were players he knew well from his youth; it was maybe even worth some money. When he got home, he showed it to his wife, also a Dodgers fan, and then put the ball on his dresser. It was largely forgotten for the next several years, until 2004.

Leland Sports Auction, based in Long Island, began posting full-page bounty posters for the missing Bobby Thomson home run ball. The company's owner, John Evans, would pay $1,000,000 for the ball. After seeing one of these ads, alarms sounded off inside Joe Biegel's head. Was the $2 ball he bought, the ball buried under junk mail and receipts on top of his dresser - was that *the* ball?

Biegel would spend the next few days doing research and trying his best to authenticate the ball himself. He didn't want to take it to the auction house president without some confidence that it could be the Bobby Thomson home run ball. He'd even go so far as to contact the Baseball Hall of Fame about whether the stamp on the ball should bear Ford Frick's signature, the commissioner of baseball at the time, or his successor, Warren Giles. The Leland ad said the ball should have Giles' stamp, but Biegel was adamant that this was an inaccuracy. The Hall of Fame agreed with him.

This signature proved to be a sticking point when he showed the ball to Mr. Evans, the man with the money for the Thomson artifact. Biegel tried to plead his case but was sent home with the Salvation Army ball still in his hand. Leland Sports Auction ultimately chose another ball and sold it for $50,000 (the chosen ball couldn't be authenticated either, but won Evans' attention).

Jack Biegel was upset by the entire situation. He wasn't confident that he had the ball, but he was certain that neither was the ball that Leland's put to auction. He turned to his son for help.

Brian Biegel was a reporter and after a few months of convincing from his father, he decided he'd use his journalistic insights to get to the bottom of the Thomson ball mystery once and for all. He'd been in a deep depression after his divorce and treated this new endeavor as a tool to regain control of his life and mental well-being.

He was beginning a quest to try and solve one of baseball's greatest mysteries and, with any luck, prove his father had the Holy Grail of baseball memorabilia, or find it along the way.

Pafko At The Wall

Brian Biegel's first stop was the Baseball Hall of Fame to examine some of the artifacts from the famous game. In a bizarre chance encounter, he bumped into Thomson's girlfriend, Esther Daniels, while viewing the exhibit. This led him to an interview with the man himself.

It seemed like the greatest start to Biegel's hunt for the famous ball. He sat down with Thomson and asked several standard interview questions. Then, he began inquiring about the ball. Thomson had little to recall about the ball after the hit. However, he did tell Biegel that a man approached him outside Yankee Stadium a few days later with the ball. The stranger told Thomson he would trade the ball for two tickets to the World Series game that afternoon.

Thomson was thrilled and raced to the clubhouse manager requesting the two tickets. When he explained why the manager just laughed and brought the home run hero to his locker. There was a stack of baseballs piled up at the bottom. They were all from people claiming to have the ball and looking for tickets or money. Throughout his life, Thomson would experience a steady stream of individuals producing the famed ball, or so they said.

This news put a twist in Biegel's stomach. How could he find a ball when there are so many copycats out there? Even if there was a way to scientifically test the balls and prove that one of them was *the* ball, it would cost a small fortune to test each one.

Biegel took a new approach. Rather than find the ball, he would try to find the person who caught the ball. This bought him to *Pafko at the Wall,* a photo printed in the *Daily Times* that showed Section 35 of the Polo Grounds moments after the ball went over the wall. He'd find another photo from a different angle taken seconds after *Pafko at the Wall.*

With the two photos in hand, Biegel enlisted the help of Dan Austin, a forensic detective retired from a career in the

NYPD. Austin and another detective scanned the pictures with magnifying glasses for some time. Their years of investigative police work quickly paid off.

When *Pafko at the Wall* first appeared in papers, the editor put in an arrow singling out one excited individual in the crowd. The editor must have assumed he was the lucky one to catch the artifact. Austin immediately disregarded this, noticing that no one else in the crowd is looking at the man. Instead, their heads are turned and looking back, suggesting the ball went further into the stands.

The team, which soon included others from Austin's contacts, analyzed the photos for weeks, even months. The most significant discovery was locating the actual ball, still in flight, in one of the photos. This changed everything. Biegel could now narrow down who possibly caught the ball to a dozen or so individuals.

Biegel took his evidence, including an enlarged photo of the select individuals in the crowd where the ball *actually* landed, and went to the media. His idea was to run the photo of the primary suspects with a hotline. The hope was that someone would recognize themselves, a friend, or a relative, in the photo.

The hope was one of these people would have a dusty old shoebox in their attic with a legendary baseball inside of it.

Lots Of Nonsense And A Nun Named Helen

Brian Biegel was successful in getting the photo published in the media. It was even published by the *Daily Times*, the same publication that ran the original story featuring the *Pafko at the Wall* picture. It didn't take long for the phone calls to come flooding in.

As expected, not all of the incoming tips on the ball were valuable, or even about the correct ball, or even baseball. The most promising lead was a woman claiming to have a Bobby Thomson ball. She was right, but it was not *the* ball. Instead, and somewhat miraculously, it was Thomson's first home run ball.

Through all the scammers and general nonsense to hit Biegel's phone, one call proved to be the lead to break everything open. The call was from a lifelong Dodgers fan claiming to have read everything written about his favorite team. He explained that a book was published in 1952 titled *Dodger Daze and Knights* that named who caught the ball.

Dodger Daze and Knights was written by Tommy Holmes, a beat reporter who was at the 1951 game. While every sportswriter at the game mobbed home plate and followed Thomson into the clubhouse, hoping to get a locker room quote to run in their headline the next morning, Holmes took a different approach. He ran across the field and into the stands, hoping to get the story from the fan who caught the ball.

This is exactly the story Holmes got. Biegel and his team now had the name of the woman who caught the ball. It actually dropped right into her lap. Her name was Helen Gawn. Biegel immediately hired a team of private detectives to track the woman down. Unfortunately, there was no Helen Gawn that fit the narrative.

With the trail cold once again, Biegel started to feel that his quest had come to an end and the mystery would remain unsolved. Once more, he would get an incredibly lucky break. Associates of Biegel's were at a local grocery store talking about sports. A stranger joined the conversation and revealed an interesting piece of information about the 1951 playoff game.

He told the group that they were standing not far from where the Bobby Thomson home run ball was, the very ball Biegel was looking for. The stranger revealed that the ball was at a convent in Lodi, New Jersey. Why was it there? Because the woman who caught it lived as a nun there. Her name was Sister Helen.

Locating Sister Helen became a challenge in itself. Not only was it difficult to get any information about her from her fellow nuns, but she had also moved from Lodi, New Jersey. Biegel would speak to a convent in Buffalo, NY, where there had been a 'Sister Helen'. And Sister Helen was known to be a baseball fan.

Unfortunately, the journey wasn't a simple trip to upstate New York. Sister Helen had moved to New Mexico, changing her name in the process to Sister Rita. It's worth mentioning that Saint Rita is the unofficial Patron Saint of baseball. This small factoid encouraged Biegel to follow the lead to its end.

The End Of A Search And A Mystery

Sister Helen died on April 14, 1990, in California, and was buried near the convent in New Mexico. Biegel was able to acquire some updated photos of Sister Helen (AKA Rita). He consulted a facial comparative analyst to use these photos against the blurry image from *Pafko at the Wall*. The analyst determined perfect matches in some areas.

It wasn't definitive, but it was promising.

When Biegel traveled to New Mexico, he sat down with the Mother Superior who knew Sister Helen. He showed her the images of *Pafko at the Wall*. The Mother Superior instantly recognized Sister Helen in the photo. It was the final validation Biegel needed. He had found the person that caught Bobby Thomson's home run ball.

Now the question was simple. Where was the ball?

After Sister Helen passed, her possessions, a shoebox worth of items, were passed to her sister Genevieve. By the time Biegel made this connection, Genevieve had also passed away. The closest relative Biegel could find was her son

(Helen's nephew) Paul. After a phone call, Biegel discovered the final fate of the ball.

On the way home from Sister Helen's funeral, Genevieve tossed the shoebox out the window and into a landfill as they passed by. Paul didn't remember if they even looked inside the box. Had they, they would have spotted a baseball, hidden for decades out of shame and sin by Sister Helen.

The search was over, and the mystery was solved, even without the ball to prove it. The hunt for the Thomson ball has many similarities to "the Shot Heard 'Round the World" itself. The Giants, despite their success against the Dodgers, did not win the World Series. They lost to the Yankees in six games. Biegel found the truth, about the ball.

However, both stories show what happens when you don't give up. The New York Giants were thought to be finished in mid-August. There was no way they could catch the Dodgers. Yet, the team kept winning and winning, down to the last game and the heroic home run by Bobby Thomson.

Biegel faced even more impossible odds. His quest to track down a ball that hadn't been seen (except by maybe its owner) in over 60 years was an impossible challenge. He faced plenty of dead ends and opportunities to throw in the towel. Like the Giants, he never did. He always remained hopeful.

Endings don't have to be perfect to be happy.

CHAPTER 6:

DEREK JETER—ROOKIE, CAPTAIN, THE FACE OF BASEBALL

There are two reasons why baseball fans remember players. The first is what they did throughout their career - the numbers, statistics, records, awards, trophies, etc. The second is *how* they played the game - their demeanor, attitude, leadership, work ethic, and so on. When it comes to Derek Jeter, he had mountains of accolades *and* the respect of the entire baseball community.

Even the fan bases that Jeter terrorized throughout his time in big leagues (Red Sox, Braves, Orioles, Indians, Athletics - it's a pretty long list) admired the must-win style of play and his demeanor on and off the field. It was why he was widely known as the face of baseball during his career. He was as much a good person as he was a tremendous baseball player. That's what earned him respect in the baseball world.

From his rookie year on, even before he was officially named team captain, he became the heartbeat of the New York Yankees. Surrounded by a core of other young talents, Jeter and the Yankees established themselves as one of baseball's greatest dynasties. Their winning mentality, driven by Jeter, helped them win games before anyone even took the field. You never felt comfortable or at ease playing the Yankees during the Jeter days.

Unraveling what made the Yankees so successful for so many years is a matter of understanding the man at the center of it all. If the Beatles were a baseball team, they would be the Yankees during the 1990s and early 2000s. Jeter was the face of the biggest team in the game and fame never seemed to impact him at all.

A Self-Fulfilling Prophecy

Some people spend an entire lifetime looking for their calling in life. This was not the case for Derek Jeter. He knew from an early age that he wanted to be a baseball player. He wanted to be the shortstop for the New York Yankees. It was the only thing he wanted to do and the only team he wanted to play for.

Growing up in Kalamazoo, Michigan was not the best environment for someone dreaming to be a professional ballplayer. Long winters and short summers left little time for baseball. There was also a general belief that players from cold-weather areas didn't face great competition. When young Derek Jeter would convey his dreams to others, they'd laugh it off. Some would even bring it up to his parents, suggesting they do a better job anchoring his goals in reality.

His parents didn't subscribe to that style of parenting advice. They told both of their children they could be anyone they want to be and to never let anyone tell them differently. "Can't" was a curse word in the Jeter household. They did, however, impress upon their children the importance of hard work. Jeter's father never let either of the kids win at anything, demonstrating that life isn't always fair, and nothing comes easily.

It instilled in young Jeter an unrelenting work ethic. When it became too cold in Kalamazoo to play outside, he would construct a hitting contraption in the garage, spending hours every day hitting off the tee. "There may be people who have more talent than you, but there's no excuse for anyone to work harder than you do," he famously said.

In high school, he made headlines as the seventh overall best high school player in the country. All Jeter could do was focus on the #1 name on the list. He didn't just want to be the best in his town or the state. He set his sights on being the best in the country. It was his first goal in baseball. By the time he was 18 and ready for the MLB draft, he was the #1 ranked high school player in the country.

When the draft came, the Houston Astros had the number one pick. Hal Newhouser recommended the team use its pick to get Derek Jeter. He felt the young shortstop was the type of talent that would be the centerpiece of any competitive team in the majors. Of course, he was right. However, the Astros front office didn't listen. Newhouser quit his job, stating that if he couldn't convince his bosses what an obvious talent Jeter was, he didn't belong in the game anymore. He retired after spending 50 years in baseball.

Jeter was drafted sixth overall by the New York Yankees, his favorite team. Three months after graduating high school, he was with some of the Yankees at a training site. The press was on him instantly, as to be expected for any first-round draft pick. At only 18, he was beyond his years regarding his attitude and demeanor toward the media.

"I'll be here in three years," Jeter confidently told the press about his timeline for becoming the Yankees' future shortstop. He was coming for the big leagues.

Not A Rookie For Long

Derek Jeter's estimated timeline for reaching the big leagues was accurate. However, it wasn't a road without obstacles. As soon as he entered the rookie leagues, the wheels began to fall off the wagon, and reality set in. He was homesick and seemed to only do wrong in the field. He racked up 56 errors in a short season. It was such a bad year it was almost impressive. It was a performance that made everyone in the Yankees organization think twice about the decision. Had they made a colossal mistake with their draft pick?

Luckily, Jeter's performance (or lack thereof) began to pick up in the 1994 season. Once he started to find success in the field and at the plate again, his confidence came back. The more confident he became, the greater his success. Pretty soon, he was running through the Yankees' farm system.

A year later, he was called up to the New York Yankees. His first game wasn't spectacular. He went 0-5 at the plate and wouldn't get his first hit until the following game. The Yankees would go to the postseason that year. While Jeter wasn't on the active roster, meaning he wasn't eligible to play, he was able to watch the games from the dugout. The Yankees would lose in the ALDS to the Seattle Mariners. Jeter's front-row view of the whole series gave him his first sense of how thrilling the playoffs were. And, how bad it felt to get so far and lose.

The 1995 year had felt like the last chance to win it all. After the season, they lost key players, like the team captain Don Mattingly, and most of the coaching staff. The newer regime of players, including Jeter, Jorge Posada, Mariano Rivera, and Bernie Williams didn't *feel* like the playoff-worthy team from a year prior. All eyes were on top draft pick Derek Jeter in Spring Training. The attention (and pressure) increased in the final week of the preseason when Tony Fernández broke his arm. Jeter was now the new everyday shortstop for the Yankees.

While his Spring Training numbers weren't great, he started to shine in his everyday role. As the season got rolling, fans and teammates watched the 21-year-old shortstop come into his own. He was making incredible plays in almost every game. Moreover, he became an energy in the clubhouse that made everyone forget the young man was only a rookie.

After clinching the division, Jeter gave another prophetic response to the press, just as he did when he predicted reaching the big leagues in three years. "We hope to celebrate three more times after every round of the playoffs and after the World Series." The Yankees indeed celebrated three more times that season, beating the Atlanta Braves in the World Series. Jeter's gutsy and aggressive play style was a critical element to the team's playoff success.

It was only the beginning.

The Captain's Dynasty

The Yankees would lose the following season (1997) in the ALDS versus Cleveland. It was that bitter feeling Jeter felt in 1995 on the bench. He found it hurt much worse when you were in the mix of players competing to win. "Once you win, there's nothing else to do but to win again. Anything less than that is a complete failure," said Jeter.

The real talks of a dynasty happened after the 1998 season. Not only did the Yankees roll through the season, winning a record-setting 114 games, but they also made a mockery of every team they faced in the postseason, including a sweep of the San Diego Padres in the World Series. It wasn't just the fact that the Yankees won games. It was this attitude that they *knew* they were going to win. Even advancing through the playoffs felt matter-of-fact to the Bronx Bombers.

It was a similar story in 1999. They didn't win as many regular season games, but they had another postseason of seemingly effortless success. They swept the Atlanta Braves in the World Series, a team with as much star-studded talent as the Yankees. The Yankees had won World Series titles in three out of four years, but the only thought on Jeter's mind was the next season and the next win.

The pressure at the start of the 2000 season was to win a third World Series in a row. It was the expectation every year - win or bust. The insistence on winning that the fans and the Yankees culture created started to wear on the players. A team that played like a runaway freight train suddenly found itself just barely limping into the playoffs. Some critics felt the young Yankees team was starting to show some age. When they faced the younger Oakland Athletics in Game Five of the ALDS that year, Eric Chavez commented before the game that it was time for another team to have some glory. It was all the motivation the Yankees needed to ignite the fire again. They finished the Athletics that day, rolled through the Mariners the next week, and completed the dynastic three-part World Series victory in a Subway Series versus the Mets.

The Yankees would reach the World Series in 2001, but lose to the Arizona Diamondbacks. It was a devastating loss, especially with the series stretching to seven games. In the wake of the September 11 attacks, Jeter and the Yankees felt like they needed to win this one more than any of the others. Coming up short was the single worst defeat in the shortstop's career. To make matters worse, many of the Yankees players were retiring or moving to other teams. It became a new chapter in the franchise's legacy.

In 2003, the Yankees ownership named Jeter the 11th captain in history. It was a nod to the work he had done so far in his career and the leadership role he would continue to play in the future of the team. It was a responsibility he took seriously for the remainder of his career as the Yankees' shortstop.

Throughout the rest of his career, he continued to be the keystone of the Yankees team. He'd even lead them to a World Series title one more time in 2009. It wasn't his performance that put him in a leadership role. It was who he was as a person, from the way he carried himself to the way he talked to teammates, executives, and even the press.

Derek Jeter inspired others without trying. His persona was contagious. He didn't have to say anything for people around him to want to do better. He had clarity of who he was and what he was there to do. That quality became a North Star for other teammates and players. His departure from baseball wasn't just a loss to the Yankees, it was a loss to the entire sport.

CHAPTER 7:

ROBERT CLEMENTE'S IMPACT ON AND OFF THE FIELD

Baseball history honors players because of their exploits on the field. You reach the Hall of Fame by being the best player, setting the best records, and helping your team win the most games. Roberto Clemente was no exception. He had the resume of a Hall of Fame player - 3,000 hits, a career .317 batting average, two World Series championships, World Series MVP honors, NL MVP, and 12-time All-Star. The list goes on.

Every Hall of Famer has a list of records and awards like Clemente's. Many have had even more impressive playing careers. Yet, Clemente's legacy often outshines these other players. He was a great baseball player, but he was also a tremendously charitable person. His humanitarian efforts and charity work are shining examples that players still use today for inspiration.

Clemente spent countless hours visiting the Children's Hospital of Pittsburgh. He would do anything to put a smile on the young patients' faces. When baseball season was over, his attention shifted to his home, Puerto Rico. He established free baseball clinics using money from his own pocket. Clemente believed every child that wanted to learn to play baseball should have the opportunity to do so.

For Clemente, his baseball career was a vehicle to help him drive his humanitarian efforts. He believed his baseball skills gave him the prosperity and opportunity to help others. He was a player and person who gave it his all, on the field and off.

A Double Minority

Roberto Clemente was a natural talent from a young age. He stood out as a track and field star as a kid, with many people feeling he was a future Olympian. Clemente had other plans and turned his attention to baseball. After playing baseball and softball during high school, he joined the Ferdinand Juncos amateur league team at 16 years old. Two years later, in 1952, he joined Puerto Rico's professional league, becoming a member of the Cangrejeros de Santurce. Clemente's island home couldn't contain his talent for long.

Al Campanis was a scout for the Los Angeles Dodgers, scouting Puerto Rico and other parts of Central America for baseball talent. Campanis was so impressed he declared Clemente was the "best free-agent athlete [he'd] ever seen." At the scout's recommendation, the Dodgers sent Clemente an impressive offer, which he accepted.

Clemente would play in the minor leagues for the Montreal Royals. The structure of the baseball draft at the time meant that Clemente didn't belong to the Dodgers organization yet. He would still be part of a draft and any team could scoop him up. The Dodgers hoped that Montreal would be a place to "hide" Clemente's talents from other scouts. He scarcely played in games or even practice with the team if other scouts were seen in the area.

The tactic didn't work.

Clyde Sukeforth of the Pittsburgh Pirates organization was viewing the Royals for a few days in 1954. He intended to evaluate Clemente's teammate Joe Black. Even though Clemente barely played, his talents were obvious to Sukeforth. He reportedly told the Royals' manager to "take good care of 'our boy' and see he didn't get hurt," referring to Clemente. A few months later, the Puerto Rican star was drafted by the Pirates. He'd debut with the Pittsburgh team the following year.

The early days of Clemente's MLB career were a tough transition. While Jackie Robinson had broken baseball's color barrier seven years prior, racism was still common. Clemente experienced it especially harshly because of his half-Black and half-Latino heritage. He endured all of the race-related language and remarks as did his Black teammates. And he was degraded for his heavy accent. When a car accident sidelined him for a few games, the press, fans, and even teammates blamed it on his "natural laziness."

Through all of this hardship, Clemente didn't waiver about his own beliefs regarding color and race. He did his best to shrug off bigoted comments and unfair snipes by the media. Rather than lash out, he used their painful and unfair words to motivate his aggressive style of play.

The Great One

By 1960, Clemente's athleticism and skills were on full display. In the early months, he was hitting .353 and batting in runs almost every game. In August, he'd make a spectacular catch, crashing into the wall, to rob Willie Mays of a hit. With the Pirates going on to win the game by just one run, Clemente's incredible defensive play was the difference maker. By the end of the year, Clemente hit above .300 and helped his team reach the World Series versus the New York Yankees.

If Clemente felt any pressure from playing in the World Series, he didn't show it. He recorded a hit in all seven games of the series, maintaining the same .300-plus average he held during the regular season. He also had three RBIs and scored a run. With how close every Pirates' win was throughout the series, these runs were all crucial contributions.

From 1960 on, Roberto Clemente was a perennial All-Star, Gold Glove winner, and .300 hitter. Only in 1968 did he fail to hit about .300 or make the All-Star roster (he still managed a Gold Glove). His consistency at the plate and in the field made him one of the best players in baseball during that time, with many adamantly declaring him the best overall.

In 1971, Clemente and the Pittsburgh Pirates made another appearance in the World Series. They faced the Baltimore

Orioles this time, a team that was coming off their third 100-win season in a row. The Orioles were also the reigning World Series champions. After losing the first two games, the Pirates had their backs against the wall. Pittsburgh held on and eventually forced a Game Seven. Clemente's defensive and offensive efforts helped keep the Pirates in the fight. His home run in Game Seven was vital to the team's 2-1 win. He was named the 1971 World Series MVP.

Clemente's last season saw him achieve his 3,000th hit. It was the last regular-season game of his life. He'd bat .247 in the playoffs, participating in his last game on October 11, 1972.

Tragedy And Legacy

Roberto Clemente Jr. was always scared when his father flew. He'd often hide the plane tickets or other essential belongings, hoping to delay his father long enough that he wouldn't have to leave. It never worked. As his grandmother, tucked him into bed and assured young Robertito that everything would be okay, the child protested. He told his grandmother he thought the plane was going to crash.

Eerily, his premonition was correct. Robert Clemente's plane, overloaded with relief supplies for victims of an earthquake in Nicaragua, crashed into the ocean shortly after takeoff. After days of searching, the world reached an unfortunate conclusion. Roberto Clemente, one of the greatest athletes and humanitarians of the time, was gone.

Clemente had decided to accompany the plane after previous attempts to get supplies to the disaster-stricken people were unsuccessful. Corrupt government officials in Nicaragua had seized or otherwise diverted the supplies elsewhere. Clemente believed taking the supplies himself would dissuade any attempts by these nefarious agents.

The tragedy of Clemente's death was a devastating blow. Puerto Rico issued three days of mourning to grieve their iconic star's passing. Puerto Ricans alive at the time remember where they were when it happened, the same way Americans remember where they were when the planes hit the World Trade Center or Kennedy was shot. There is now an official Roberto Clemente holiday in Puerto Rico.

The Baseball Hall of Fame fast-tracked Clemente's entry. Typically, players had to wait years after their careers to be eligible. He was only the second player in history to have this waiting period waived and the first Latino player ever inducted. In another honor, MLB named an award in his honor. The Robert Clemente Award is given to a player each year who exemplifies Clemente's performance on and off the field. Willie Stargell, a fellow Pittsburgh Pirate, won the award in 1974, picking up the mantle of his teammate's hard work and humanitarian efforts.

The inspirational takeaway of Clemente's legacy is best summed up by the man himself, "Any time you have an opportunity to make a difference in this world and you don't, then you are wasting your time on Earth." Seize every opportunity, great or small, and make a difference in the lives of those around you.

CHAPTER 8:

BASEBALL HELPS AMERICA GET BACK ON ITS FEET AFTER SEPTEMBER 11

Baseball is known as "America's Pastime." Yet, the reasoning behind this prestigious title is sometimes lost on today's audiences. Baseball's history and the history of the country have always run parallel to one another, and at times they cross paths in meaningful and profound ways. This is particularly true during times of war and tragedy.

As America entered World War II, many of baseball's best athletes were called to service: Hank Greenberg, Warren Spahn, Bob Feller, Ted Williams, and Yogi Berra, just to name a few. The game saw its brightest stars disappearing from starting lineups and appearing on draft boards. It made many people question whether baseball would continue at all, which prompted President Franklin Delano Roosevelt to write a letter to the decision-makers of Major League Baseball:

> *What I am going to say is solely a personal and not an official point of view. I honestly feel that it would be best for the country to keep baseball going. There will be fewer people unemployed and everybody will work longer hours and harder than ever before. And that means that they ought to have a chance for recreation and for taking their minds off their work even more than before.*

FDR felt baseball was a necessity because of its ability to distract the American people from the atrocities happening overseas. It was a needed leisure at a time when nothing felt fun or cheerful. Baseball has continued to be that positive force during the darkest times in American history. This remained true in the wake of the terrorist attacks on September 11.

A Date Which Will Live In Infamy

On the morning of December 7, 1941, the Japanese air military surprise attacked the US naval base at Pearl Harbor. The event prompted America's entry into World War II. FDR called the attacks on Pearl Harbor "a date which will live in infamy," when he addressed congress and urged them to declare war on Japan and the other members of the Axis Powers.

Sixty years later, America faced another date that will forever be remembered in US history books. Nineteen terrorists hijacked four commercial flights in a planned assault on the American people. Two planes were crashed into the World Trade Center in New York City and a third hit the Pentagon in Virginia. The fourth plane crashed into a field after the passengers onboard bravely overcame the hijackers.

The attacks stunned the nation. On the day of the terrorist event, everything came to a screeching halt. The entire country watched on TV as the events unfolded and the Twin Towers collapsed. While the attacks happened exclusively in the northeast, and with most of the destruction occurring in

New York City, the entire country felt as if there was a hole in the center of everything.

It was the first time since Pearl Harbor in 1941 that America was attacked on its own home field. It was unexpected, tragic, alarming, and deadly. It felt like life would never return to normalcy.

Baseball commissioner Bud Selig promptly postponed every game on September 11. Later, he would cancel the remaining games for the rest of the week. The plan was to resume play at the start of the following week. Security was heightened at every ballpark.

With everything else happening around the country and in New York City, the fate of the baseball season seemed irrelevant. However, the actions of the baseball community in the days that followed the attacks, especially by the New York Mets and New York Yankees, became a significant remedy to the woes of the American people.

Baseball provided - if only for a moment - a distraction from all the hurt and anger felt from coast to coast.

The New York Yankees

When the attacks occurred, the New York Yankees were slated to play a doubleheader in New York against the Chicago White Sox. Yankees catcher, Jorge Posada, was at NYU Hospital with his son Jorge Jr., doing his best to distract the youngster before surgery. He caught glimpses of the World Trade Center on TV screens throughout the hospital and noticed nurses frantically rushing about. He didn't yet understand the full catastrophe of the situation.

Posada placed a call to teammate Derek Jeter, asking the star shortstop to let him know about the games later because something had happened at the World Trade Center. When Jeter awoke and turned on his TV, he saw what the rest of the world was watching. New York City, the city he called home, had been attacked.

While no games were played, the Yankees still met for workouts and training. On September 15, after one of these workouts, manager Joe Torre and some of the Yankees players, including Jeter and center fielder Bernie Williams, went to the heart of tragedy.

Their first visit was uneasy. What could they, a group of baseball players, possibly do in the throngs of emergency workers, grieving families, and victims? These apprehensions quickly faded once they began meeting people. Joe Torre describes their feelings in *The Yankee Years*:

> *I think I realized at that point in time there was a purpose for us being there…We sort of just walked in there and looked around. And then somebody looked up and sort of waved us in, a family member. They*

brought out pictures of the family members they were waiting on, pictures of them wearing Yankees hats.

Williams walked up to a distraught woman at the scene and simply said, "I don't know what to say, but you look like you need a hug." The embrace was a small but meaningful gesture that immediately changed how the Yankees felt about their role in all of this chaos and hurt. They didn't have the tools to treat physical injuries or pull survivors from the wreckage of the Twin Towers. What they did have was the power to connect with New Yorkers, make them smile for just a moment, and, if only briefly, forget about their pain.

The Yankees would resume their baseball schedule by playing the White Sox in Chicago. Fans at the game displayed a large banner that read "Chicago ♡ N.Y., God Bless America." When the Yankees took the field as the away team, the Chicago fans gave them a standing ovation. The same level of energy would greet the Yankees when they returned to their home crowd. Derek Jeter recalled the emotions of playing baseball after the attacks:

It was almost an uncomfortable feeling for all of us when we first got back to playing baseball. The thing that we figured out was, even if it was for a short period of time, three hours a day, we gave people something to cheer for. We felt as though we were playing for more than ourselves. We felt as though we were playing for all of New York.

Joe Torre echoed these thoughts: "I never realized how important baseball was until 9/11."

Mike Piazza Hits The Biggest Home Run Of His Career

Three days after the Yankees played the game in Chicago, the New York Mets, wearing NYPD and NYFD hats, hosted their divisional rival, the Atlanta Braves, at Shea Stadium. It was the first sporting event to occur on the battered New York soil.

With Shea Stadium adorned in red, white, and blue, the opening ceremonies began. As the camera panned down the line of Mets players, catcher Mike Piazza was one of the most visibly affected by the moving moments unfolding. He had no idea that he was about to hit one of the most impactful home runs in baseball and American history.

Through the first few innings, there was just a baseball game going on. It might have distracted fans a little bit, but there was still a melancholy air permeating throughout the stadium. There were even concerns that such a gathering of people would be a target of another attack.

In the fourth inning, each team scored a run, sparking a little life in the crowd before it returned to a quiet game again. Both pitchers were throwing well. John Franco managed to outlast Jason Marquis, the Braves starter. But he ran into trouble in the eighth inning. After putting baserunners on, Armando Benitez came in to relieve Franco. He gave up a double and the Braves were suddenly ahead.

The Mets came to bat in the bottom of the eighth. Steve Karsay, the Braves pitcher and a New York City native himself, got a quick out before walking Edgardo Alfonzo. Suddenly, Mike Piazza was at the plate, representing the go-ahead run. He was just who Mets fans wanted to see at such a critical moment.

The crowd began to chant. "Let's go, Mets! Let's go, Mets!" Every utterance of this phrase shouted into the New York air at Shea Stadium began to wash away the collective hurt, replacing it with joy and jubilation.

Piazza didn't bite at the first pitch. He rarely did - a batting quirk he was known for. On the second pitch, Karsay was hoping Piazza would chase a pitch off the plate. He missed the target and left it right over the plate. Piazza loaded and swung.

Crack!

Some hits in baseball just sound pure. You know it's a home run just by the sound of it. Mike Piazza's hit that night rang true. The 41,000 people in attendance watched it sail over the left-center wall before disappearing into the camera tower. Shea Stadium erupted. "It was just this incredible release of emotion," Mike Piazza said later.

Mets fans were smiling. People who had lost loved ones. Firefighters that had spent days pulling victims from the tangled rubble of the towers. Emergency workers that had to tell families that their loved ones weren't coming home. They were all smiling, embracing, cheering, and celebrating. They were experiencing happiness for the first time in too long.

The Mets went on to win the game. The victory didn't belong to the Mets. It was a win for all of New York City. It was a moment of triumph over suffering. Mike Piazza and the Mets helped heal the city that night.

Baseball is just a game, as simple as a bat and ball, but its effect on the American people in the weeks after the terrorist attacks of September 11 was transcendent. It was a power as profound as the American spirit it helped restore.

CHAPTER 9:

TED WILLIAMS, THE SPLENDID SPLINTER, FIGHTS TWO WARS AND BATS .406

Ted Williams' baseball career started in 1939 and ended in 1960. Throughout that time, he played in almost 20 baseball seasons and fought in two different wars. Adolf Hitler was celebrating his 50th birthday the day Ted Williams joined the Boston Red Sox. On his last day, Americans were reading about Nixon and JFK's first TV debate.

He was the last hitter to hit over .400 in a season and has the best career batting average of the live-ball era. He is a popular choice for the title of greatest hitter of all time. He could hit towering home runs and torpedo line drives seemingly at will.

After his best hitting season (1941), where Williams would reach a .406 batting average over 456 ABs, the United States entered World War II. A few months later, Ted Williams enlisted in the Navy and became a pilot, effectively putting his baseball career on pause.

At the start of 1952, Williams' baseball career would be interrupted once more by military duty. He was called to serve in the Korean War. While he didn't see any action in World War II, he did in Korea. He even experienced a crash landing. Yet, the Splendid Splinter, as he was known, survived and returned to baseball.

It's hard to theorize how good of a player Ted Williams *could* have been, had his baseball career not been interrupted by service in the military. After all, he was one of the best to play the game even with the temporary pauses. He seemed to never lose his natural talent or his drive to be the greatest hitter of all time.

Master Of Everything

When a pitcher strikes out a batter, it feels like a small win. You beat the hitter in a one-on-one contest. Striking out Ted Williams, on the other hand, made pitchers feel like they got away with one, like it shouldn't have happened but did. They got lucky. That's how good of a hitter he was.

Any player as good as Williams has some raw talent consisting of intangible qualities that other players lack to such a high degree. For Ted, it was his eyes and his brain - the two most crucial bodily instruments for baseball players. It was these tools that led him to such great success at the plate and also as a pilot in the air.

His eyes weren't just tools at the plate to see incoming pitches. Williams was a student of the game of baseball. He watched *everything*. He studied pitchers to look for weaknesses or tells that would reveal which pitch was coming. By the time he got to the plate, he knew what pitches to expect, where the pitcher liked to throw them, and when. He knew the pitcher's sequences, tendencies, and patterns. Williams had the advantage before a single pitch was thrown.

He also watched and talked to other hitters, looking for any useful insights to help him improve his own game. If a player had an unorthodox stance or swing, Williams needed to know why. It was this attention to detail, his curiosity, and a pure passion for being the best that made him a success in every capacity of his life.

Teammate Johnny Pesky saw firsthand what a natural talent Williams was when they went into aviation training together. While both men were high school graduates, Pesky was at a clear disadvantage when it came to studying and learning. Meanwhile, Williams seemed to master complicated concepts and training programs in just a fraction of the time of others. The brain that had been processing batting techniques and pitches for years was now fixed on aviation drills and college courses.

It wasn't just that Ted Williams was smart. He was hungry for information. A business partner later in Williams' life explained his thirst for knowledge. "You'd see him one day and talk about some subject he didn't know. The next day, he'd bring up the same subject, and he'd know more about it than you did."

This anecdote highlights what made Williams so brilliant at everything he did. He was never satisfied with being average or "okay" at something. No matter what skill or interest lay in front of him, from baseball and golf to piloting and current events, Williams put in the work to be exceptional. His successes were 10% natural talent and 90% hard work and studying.

Military Service

Ted Williams had obvious talent in the cockpit. According to Johnny Pesky, "Ted could make a plane, and its six [machine guns] play like a symphony…His reflexes, coordination, and visual reaction made him a built-in part of the machine." Yet, he would never see combat in World War II.

He spent most of his time during the war in Pensacola, Florida. This is where he finished his advanced flight training and moved up to the rank of second lieutenant. He stayed in Pensacola to train other young pilots. His skills in the cockpit made him a great learning tool for others, even with his short temper.

When the war ended, he was in Hawaii, stationed at Pearl Harbor. He was supposed to report to combat in the Pacific, but the war ended before he got his orders. The star of the Boston Red Sox was released from service soon after. He would stay in the Marine Corps Reserve.

Staying an active member of the Marine Corps Reserve earned him the title of Captain. When the Korean War started, Williams was called back to duty. He had the option to join a baseball team of servicemen, which would have been a comfortable (and safe) position. He declined and opted to be a pilot again. Williams had not flown in eight years.

Much of his World War II pilot training went out the window. These weren't the propeller antiques Williams was used to. He had to quickly train and study up on the new F-9 Panther jets. These new planes were faster and more sophisticated. Williams was a quick learner.

His lack of action in World War II was the opposite of his experiences in Korea. He saw almost immediate combat and would fly in almost 40 air combat missions throughout the war. Ironically, his first mission was his most dangerous.

He participated in a massive raid about 15 miles south of Pyongyang, the capital of North Korea. Initially, everything went according to plan. He dropped his explosive payload and began pulling up to safety. Suddenly, Williams began to experience problems with his controls. His radio was dead. The stick began shaking. Indicator lights flashed in front of him.

Luckily, a 22-year-old fellow pilot named Larry Hawkins spotted the trouble. The first sign of concern was Williams was flying north, toward the capital of North Korea and more enemy artillery. Hawkins maneuvered his plane all around Williams, looking for a source of the problem. He spotted it; Williams' plane was hit.

With the guidance of Hawkins, communicating only by hand signals because of Williams' bad radio, the baseball player pilot was able to make it back to base. However, before he could land safely, the real calamity struck.

Williams' plane was smoking and leaking fuel. When he opened the doors for his landing gear, the oxygen caused the smoking fuel to combust. His plane was suddenly on fire.

Hawkins immediately began signaling for Williams to eject. Ted didn't want to eject and for good reason. Ejection seats were a new technology and not an immediately successful one. Given his tall frame, Williams was worried he'd break his legs (or worse) if he tried to eject. He was determined to land the plane, fire or not.

He hit the end of the runway and immediately began skidding across the tarmac at high speeds. He had no way to slow the plane down except press the brakes as hard as he could. He'd actually sprained his ankle from pressing so hard. He and the plane ground along the pavement before coming to a stop at the far end of the runway.

Williams jumped free of the wreckage and ran to safety. From Hawkins' vantage point, he was sure the ballplayer had jumped off the burning plane before it even came to a stop.

It was a harrowing event and just one of many missions for Williams. Roughly six months later, the left fielder for the Boston Red Sox returned home safe and sound.

A Career Of Perfection

When Williams returned home from service in the Korean War, he found himself in Tom Yawkey's office, the Boston Red Sox owner. After some back-and-forth, Yawkey convinced Williams to take some batting practice. The stadium was practically empty aside from a few players practicing before the day's game.

The returning veteran hit a couple of balls. Then, the show began. Williams found a groove and started hitting home run after home run. It was only batting practice, but he impressively launched nine balls over the fence in a row. Afterward, he approached Joe Cronin, the general manager, and asked what they did to home plate. Cronin wasn't sure what he meant. Nothing was different, he thought. Williams protested, saying the plate was crooked. A surveyor came to the field and measured home plate. It was an inch off.

Ted Williams was the only player on the planet that would notice such a minuscule detail. It was yet another example of the hitter's incredible ability to spot details that no one else could see. It's what made him such an incredible force at the plate.

Tim Horgan, a sportswriter, once interviewed a blind man who loved to come to the ballpark. Hogan asked what was so enjoyable for the man, considering he couldn't see any of the action. The man replied that he could tell what was happening by the sounds. Ted Williams was his favorite player. He knew when he was coming up to bat because the entire sound of the stadium would change. The sound of the ball off his bat was different from any other player.

It's these stories that paint the picture of Ted Williams as the greatest hitter of all time. "Baseball is the only field of endeavor where a man can succeed three times out of ten and be considered a good performer," Williams famously once said. This is a quote that has stood the test of time and is often referenced by other baseball professionals.

If you're batting over the .300 mark, you are one of the best that year, likely an all-star. Maintain a .300 average for most of your career and you'll be in the Hall of Fame. Ted Williams had a career batting average of .344. That puts him tenth overall (Ty Cobb is first with a career batting average of .366). The reason that many consider Williams to be the best to ever do it has a lot to do with *when* he played.

As a whole, baseball players have become better over time. This makes competition stiffer and hitting, especially for average, much more difficult. That's why few players have come close to Williams' 1941 record of .406. Tony Gwynn would come close in 1994 (.394).

Within the last 20 years, only eight players have hit above .350: Ichiro (three times), Joe Mauer, Chipper Jones, Magglio Ordóñez, Barry Bonds, Josh Hamilton, Albert Pujoles (twice), and Todd Helton. In the last *ten* years, no hitter has batted above this mark, demonstrating the increasing difficulty of the game over time.

Thus, many baseball experts question whether Ted Williams' .406 season batting average will ever be surpassed again. You could argue that he came as close to a perfect hitting season as imaginable in present times.

You can't sum up the inspirational impact of Williams' career with a single thing. It wasn't just his hitting or his drive to serve his country during times of war. It wasn't his attitude or tenacity on the field. It was the combined effort of a lifetime of studying the game and the world around him and finding ways to improve. He wasn't satisfied with good or great. He strived to be as perfect as possible.

Williams knew there was no such thing as a perfect baseball player. There's no such thing as a perfect player in *any* sport. Everyone misses a goal, strikes out, makes an error, or stumbles from time to time. But if we consider a .300 hitter to be great - worthy of all-star or Hall of Fame status - then Theodore Samuel Williams was as close to perfection as we may ever see again.

CHAPTER 10:

THE ROAD TO ADAM GREENBERG'S FIRST "TRUE" MAJOR LEAGUE AT BAT

Baseball is full of haves and have-nots. The haves are players you know well. They played for many seasons and did great things in their careers. The have-nots are less memorable. They may have only played for a season or two. Some of the have-nots only got a handful of at-bats. Yet, when you consider that, in the 150 years of organized baseball, only around 20,000 people have *ever played* in at least one game, having even a single at-bat on your resume is something to gloat about.

If you look at Adam Greenberg's career stats, you'd certainly jump to the conclusion that he was in the have-not category.

Year	Team	GP	AB	R	H	RBI	BB	SO	HR	SB
2012	Marlins	1	1	0	0	0	0	1	0	0
2005	Cubs	1	0	0	0	0	0	0	0	0
Career		2	1	0	0	0	0	1	0	0

It's definitely not a Hall of Fame career. It's barely a career at all. Yet, Adam Greenberg's story is an inspiring one. He fought, against all odds, to get just one at-bat, which is more than most people can say about their baseball careers.

July 9, 2005: A Start And End Of A Career

Adam Greenberg was in a Days Inn on July 7, waiting with a teammate for a phone call. The call would determine if the two players would rejoin their Cubs-affiliated Double-A team in Florida, or move up to the Cubs' Triple-A organization. When the call came, they were told to prepare for a flight to Florida. The two teammates groaned, thinking their hopes of moving up to the next tier were on hold.

There was a catch.

Greenberg and his teammate were not headed to Florida to meet back up with their Double-A team. They were going to Florida because the Chicago Cubs were playing the Florida Marlins. The two men were going to be attending their first Major League Baseball game as players.

The trip to Florida included a first-class flight and a bottle of expensive champagne waiting in Greenberg's hotel room when he landed. In the minors, Greenberg never unpacked his suitcase. He'd take out what clothes and comforts he needed at the time, leaving the rest in his bag. This time, he made sure to unpack the suitcase entirely, signaling to the universe he was here to stay.

On July 9, in the ninth inning, Greenberg got the call to pinch-hit for the pitcher. The walk to the plate was the result of years of practice, dedication, and hard work. Since he was a child, this was his dream. It was finally in front of him. He stepped into the batter's box and Marlins' pitcher Valerio de los Santos threw the first pitch.

The pitch was a wild fastball that came straight for Greenberg's head. The speed of the pitch left him with nowhere to go and no time to get out of its way. By the time Greenberg's brain realized where the ball was headed, all he could do was turn his face away. The ball hit the batting helmet just below his ear. The protective headgear actually popped off as a result of the impact.

The noise of the ball hitting the helmet sounded like a gunshot in Greenberg's ear. He fell to the ground disoriented and in pain. He clutched his skull, trying to hold the pieces together because he thought his head had split open. The trainers rushed to his aid, asking the usual questions. When they asked him where he was two days ago, Greenberg replied, "The minor leagues and I'm not going back there." The trainers laughed, helped him to his feet, and escorted him back to the dugout.

The scary moment was over, and Greenberg was seemingly okay.

More Than A Concussion

Greenberg stayed in the clubhouse for the remainder of the game. He never even needed to be hospitalized. It was a close call, but he thought he was fine. The real trouble began the next morning. He found himself unable to be around bright lights. His appetite wasn't the same. While it was concerning, most of the trainers and doctors he consulted chalked it up to a mild concussion. In a few days, the symptoms would be gone, they promised.

Since he was unable to handle being in the dugout for the games, he traveled back to his family's Connecticut home to recover. One afternoon, while laying down for a nap, Greenberg experienced something alarming. His eyes fluttered from side to side uncontrollably, followed by an intense migraine that lasted several hours.

Greenberg's entire perception of his injury changed that day. He stopped thinking about when he'd be ready to return to the Cubs. Now he was questioning whether or not he was ever going to feel normal again.

His symptoms only got worse. He experienced double vision, more migraines, loss of balance, dizzying vertigo, sensitivity to lights, and more. Every day was a nightmare for the player. He couldn't get a full night's sleep. There were stretches where he began to feel well, but another fit of vertigo would sideline him once again. He kept questioning whether this was his life from now on.

Eventually, the symptoms lessened enough that he could return to the minor leagues. He was not quite the same player who debuted for the Cubs in July. He batted only .209 the next season. It wasn't enough to keep his spot. A year later, he was out of the minor leagues. His MLB career was over after just one pitch. It wasn't even an official at-bat because he was hit by the ball.

Greenberg would continue playing baseball. He signed with the Bridgeport Bluefish, an independent league team less than an hour from his hometown of Guilford, Connecticut. He played well for the Bluefish, setting single-season records for steals and triples and becoming the team's career leader for triples. His professional baseball career was in the rearview mirror.

A Campaign For One At-Bat

While Adam Greenberg was grinding in the independent league, a faithful group of fans, led by sports documentarian Matt Liston, began a quest to get him his first at-bat. They wanted to see the former Cub get a shot at redemption. Greenberg was on board. "I've never given up," he said. "I want to prove it to myself and everyone else on the field. I just need the shot - that chance - to do it."

Liston planned to start petitioning for Greenberg, building as much buzz as possible for the now-30-year-old player. He knew it would be a long shot, but Greenberg had already defied the odds once by reaching the big leagues. Who was to say it couldn't happen a second time? Liston did everything to generate attention for Greenberg's campaign - handing out posters to baseball fans on the streets, getting on talk shows, and creating social media pages.

The movement grew from Chicago to other fanbases and quickly became a topic familiar to baseball audiences of all allegiances. Cubs GM Jed Hoyer responded to the campaign and Liston, promising to take a look at getting Greenberg his at-bat. "We owe it to him," he said.

Ultimately, Greenberg's chance didn't come in a Chicago Cubs uniform. Instead, it was the Miami Marlins who gave him his redemption opportunity. It was partly an apology for their pitcher being the one who derailed Greenberg's career. The other reason was trying to reverse a slew of negative PR facing the team's management. They were also having a 93-loss season. No matter what the reasoning, Greenberg was finally getting his first at-bat.

On October 12, 2012, seven years after he was hit by a pitch that ended his MLB career, Adam Greenberg was back in the box. His opportunity came in the sixth inning as the Marlins faced the Mets. The at-bat didn't last long. R.A. Dickey threw three straight knuckleballs for strikes. Greenberg was out, but he got his at-bat.

It may not have been the fairy tale ending that everyone wanted, but, for Greenberg, it was one of the best experiences of his life. It made his career. In the aftermath, some critics would argue that it was all a PR stunt and his three-pitch out proved that Greenberg wasn't a true MLB player. He was. He never stopped playing baseball and he was ready for the opportunity. R.A. Dickey was the 2012 Cy Young award winner. He was the best pitcher in the league. He struck out *a lot* of batters, some of them on three pitches.

Greenberg earned his ticket in 2005 and earned a shot at redemption in 2012. Greenberg experienced the highest point of his life and the lowest in the same instance. Then, he battled back and, with some help from Liston's campaign, got a second chance. Through his determination to never give up, he is one of the lucky few who can say they had an at-bat in a Major League Baseball game. He faced the game's best pitcher. He experienced a crowd giving him a standing ovation. He was a professional baseball player.

CHAPTER 11:

PETE GRAY TRIUMPHS OVER TRAGEDY

Deion Sanders is one of the best examples of a pure athlete. When he attended college at Florida State University, he played defense for the football team, outfield for the baseball team, and also participated in track events. These teams were competitive and frequently won conference or championship titles during Sanders' time at FSU.

He would go on to play in the NFL and MLB *at the same time*, meaning there were times when he was hitting home runs and scoring touchdowns in the same week! The overlap of the two professional seasons left him with little recovery or vacation time. It was go, go, go all year round!

Sanders didn't just *play* these two sports. He *excelled* at both. He's one of a small group of two-way starting players in the NFL, meaning he played both offense *and* defense. In baseball, he managed to help his team, the Atlanta Braves, reach the World Series in 1992. While they ended up losing, Sanders posted impressive numbers.

In short, only a handful of athletes are so successful at multiple sports. When Sanders was asked which one was the hardest to play, Sanders said baseball without any hesitation. "That ball does some things to you," he commented about how difficult it is to hit a baseball. "That's a hard sport."

Now, imagine playing this incredibly challenging sport with one arm. Well, that's exactly what faced Pete Gray during his baseball career.

Pete Gray's Ambition

Pete Gray grew up wanting to be a baseball player. It's an ambition shared by millions of youths across the country and the world. "I can't remember when I haven't had an ambition to be a ballplayer," he once said. "Being a big leaguer is just something I dreamed of." That dream took an unexpected and painful turn when Gray was six-years-old.

While riding on the back of a produce wagon, Gray fell. His right arm tangled in the wheel spokes and was mutilated beyond repair. His arm had to be amputated above the elbow. The injury was an immediate blow to Gray and his baseball dreams, as he was a natural right-hander.

As you often see in inspirational stories, Gray's drive and ambition were somehow bigger than the obstacles he now faced. He didn't want anyone feeling sorry for him or treating him differently because of his amputated arm. Besides, he had bigger things to worry about, like training himself to be a lefty.

Gray would train and play sandlot baseball whenever he could as a youth. He removed the inner padding from his baseball glove because it was easier for him to retrieve a ball from within the pocket. It also made the glove thinner and easier to tuck under his amputated arm when he needed to make a throw.

His first job in baseball was as a team mascot for a local semi-pro team. It wasn't exactly the position he wanted to play. No matter where he went, players and coaches scoffed at his abilities. They couldn't look beyond his single arm. Why would they hire Gray when there were plenty of good, two-armed players available?

It was a sentiment the ambitious ballplayer would hear again and again. Gray once tried to get a tryout with the last-place Athletics, thinking he could help them win more games. Manager Connie Mack responded by saying, "Son, I've got men with two arms who can't play this game." He received a less polite response when he tried to attend the Phillies' summer training camp in Miami. "Get off the field, Wingy," shouted manager Doc Prothro.

Gray's first semi-pro contract was the result of him betting on himself. He handed the team's owner a $10 bill (equivalent to over $200 today), telling the man to keep it if he didn't make good on his talents. He hit a home run in his first game.

His talents quickly won over everyone. Not only was he an incredibly fast runner, but he had trained his body and reflexes to make up for his physical disability. He had taught himself to bat one-handed, building enough strength in his left arm to swing a 38oz bat with ease. He had also devised a method of fielding and throwing. He would catch the ball with his gloved left hand and then stick the ball and glove under his amputated right arm, letting the ball drop into his now-bare left hand. The motion became so quick that there was almost no delay in his ability to catch and throw.

Gray would go on to experience a successful career in semi-pro baseball. He routinely hit above .300 and recorded a handful of one-armed home runs. Gray even made MVP honors in one season playing for the Memphis Chickasaws. These successes undoubtedly felt good for the man, but his dreams of making it to the big leagues were still unfulfilled.

World history was about to change that.

World War Ii Helps Gray's Dream Come True

It's hard to fathom that a world war had a positive impact on someone's hopes and dreams. World War II was full of unthinkable atrocities, death, destruction, and all other manners of evil and chaos. However, if there was any silver lining to be found in the turmoil, the war provided Gray with his opportunity to play baseball in the big leagues, just as he always dreamed.

World War II required many of the game's best players to pause their baseball careers and head overseas, whether by choice or via the draft. Gray himself tried to enlist after Pearl Harbor. He was denied due to his amputated arm. "If I could teach myself how to play baseball with one arm, I sure as heck could handle a rifle."

While his childhood injury would prevent him from going to war, it would no longer hinder his chances to play baseball at the highest professional level. With so many team rosters full of holes left by players heading overseas, Gray and many other hopeful and talented athletes finally got their opportunities.

The St. Louis Browns (present-day Baltimore Orioles) bought his minor league contract for $20,000. The sum and the player's obvious handicap created lots of scrutiny from his new teammates and coaches. Before even seeing him play, he was labeled as an attraction - something to sell more tickets until the war was over.

Gray, on the other hand, was determined to let his abilities do the talking, not his disability. His best day came during a doubleheader versus the Yankees. He would reach base five times on four hits and record two RBIs. His performance garnered him national attention as "Baseball's Miracle Man," or "The One-Armed Wonder," depending on who was reporting the story.

The sensationalism building around his playing only furthered his teammates' attitudes that he was an attraction to build ticket sales. Though, some players began to see what a great ballplayer he was. "I was sure when I came here this guy wasn't going to be with us long. Now I'm not so sure…I see him doing things out there I didn't think he could."

The publicity regarding his handicap created a lot of good for thousands of veterans returning from war, many of them amputees as well. Gray's baseball career became a positive light. He did what he could to respond to mail from servicemen and speak to other amputees. Although, he was quick to dispel any notions that he was courageous, even after getting an award for such from the Philadelphia Sports Writers. "Courage belongs on the battlefield, not on the baseball diamond," he said.

Unfortunately, Gray's career in professional baseball didn't last long. Major League Baseball's elite pitchers quickly found a weakness in his hitting. Due to his one-armed swing, Gray couldn't easily check his swing. Pitchers began throwing him sharp breaking balls because he couldn't edit his timing mid-swing or stop himself from chasing a bad pitch.

Moreover, with World War II drawing to an end, the game's typical stars returned home ready to play. He'd play a few more years in the minor leagues before returning home. While there was some public interest in Gray's life over the years, he avoided the attention and stayed private. He died in 2002, but not before he taught the baseball world an important lesson. With enough determination, you can be a great ballplayer, even after so much has been taken from you.

CHAPTER 12:

JACKIE ROBINSON CHANGES BASEBALL AND AMERICA

When you learn about the Civil Rights Movement in school, many inspirational heroes take center stage - Dr. Martin Luther King Jr., W.E.B. Du Bois, Rosa Parks, and Thurgood Marshall. You learn about sit-ins and walkouts, *Brown v. Board of Education,* and other pivotal events. You read Dr. King's famous *I Have a Dream* speech.

While all these people and events are crucial to the Civil Rights Movement, one critical piece is missing. It's the event and person that set the stage. It's the inspirational story of Jackie Robinson signing with the Brooklyn Dodgers, taking the field, and effectively ending baseball's longstanding color barrier that barred non-White players from entering organized baseball.

The impact and significance of this event are often underappreciated. Not only did Jackie Robinson break baseball's color barrier at a time when the sport was at the forefront of American culture, but the event preceded every significant step in the Civil Rights Movement.

Jackie Robinson taking the field in 1947 came seven years before the Supreme Court would reach its decision on *Brown V. Board of Education*. It'd be another year after that for Rosa Parks to make her stand on a city bus in Montgomery, Alabama.

To put it into further context, Dr. Martin Luther King Jr. was only 16 years old when Robinson signed his contract. It'd be another 18 years before King would make his famous speech.

Most timelines depicting the Civil Rights Movement begin with either Present Truman ending segregation in the US Military in 1948 or the ending of segregation in public schools (1954). It *really* started in 1945, with Branch Rickey and Jackie Robinson's "Great Experiment," almost two decades before the Civil Rights Act would finally pass.

Branch Rickey's "Great Experiment"

Buck O'Neil was a former baseball player and one of the many African-American stars restricted by the color of their skin to never set foot in organized baseball. In 1945, he was serving on an Army base in the Philippines when a call came that he must report to an officer's quarters at once.

There were hundreds of possible reasons bombarding O'Neil's thoughts as to why he was being called at such a late hour. Nothing he imagined could have come close to the true reason for the late-night call.

O'Neil was about to be told that Branch Rickey, owner of the Brooklyn Dodgers, had signed Jackie Robinson, an African-American, to an organized baseball contract. Overwhelmed with joy and disbelief, O'Neil snatched the microphone for the PA system and relayed the news across the rest of the base.

His disbelief was for good reason. While there was never an official rule barring African-Americans from organized baseball, team owners and the game's commissioner, Kenesaw Mountain Landis, did everything to keep the sport 'white'. As long as Landis was in office, it seemed unfathomable that an African-American player would ever play on an organized baseball team.

Landis died in November of 1944 and his successor, Albert "Happy" Chandler, proved to be a more enlightened commissioner. When pressed about permitting Blacks to play in organized baseball, he replied, "If a black boy can make it on Okinawa and Guadalcanal, he can make it in baseball." Chandler recognized the hypocrisy of segregating baseball in America, while the country was fighting a war founded in racism and antisemitism.

The rest of baseball's executives didn't agree with Chandler. A vote revealed that 15 of 16 owners were against integration. The lone supporter was Branch Rickey. The reasons that motivated Rickey to sign Jackie Robinson are often debated. Rickey was as fierce a businessman as he was a baseball executive. He understood the financial power of hiring an African-American player. The Negro Leagues were already a huge success. Games saw attendance from thousands of African-American baseball fans. Rickey hoped signing Jackie Robinson would bring this audience (and their money) to Ebbets Field, the home stadium for the Brooklyn Dodgers.

The other reason was to utilize Jackie Robinson's talents to help the Dodgers win more baseball games. "The greatest untapped reservoir of raw material in the history of our game is the black race," he once said. While baseball minds of the time scoffed at the idea of Black players outperforming White stars, the numbers painted a different story. Negro League teams held their own against professional teams, even versus lineups featuring All-Star players. They didn't just compete; they won more games than their all-White counterparts.

Rickey's faith also motivated him to introduce Robinson and Black players to organized baseball. He was a devout Christian Methodist, taking his religion so seriously he once said that his mission in life was to be "a consistent Christian and a consistent ballplayer." These beliefs caused him to question the morality of segregation in the game he loved so much. "I cannot face my God much longer knowing that his black creatures are held separate and distinct from his white creatures in the game that has given me all that I call my own."

While Jackie Robinson would face discrimination, racist insults, and other wrongdoings on the field, Rickey would face plenty of the same behind closed doors and in the press. Despite these aggressors, Rickey's faith and devotion kept him on the correct path. "Someday, I'm going to have to have to stand before God and if He asks me why I didn't let that Robinson fellow play ball, I don't think saying 'because of the color of his skin' would be a good enough answer."

The Perfect Player For The "Great Experiment"

Arguably, Rickey's "Great Experiment," as he would come to call it, was a plan in the works for decades. It began in 1903 when Rickey was the baseball coach at Ohio Wesleyan University. Charles Thomas was the catcher for the team and the only Black player. After playing a game against Notre Dame, the team arrived at their hotel. A problem quickly arose. The clerk refused to grant a room to Thomas because the establishment had a Whites-only policy. After some negotiating, Thomas was allowed to stay in Coach Rickey's room on a cot.

Later that evening, Rickey would find his young, African-American catcher sobbing in their room. Rubbing his arms and hands in a hysterical, crazed manner, he said, "It's my skin, Mr. Rickey. If it weren't for my skin, I wouldn't be any different from anyone; if only my hands were white."

The words of Thomas and the vision of him trying to tear his own skin off to be like his white teammates would rattle inside Rickey's mind for years. All he needed to fix it was to find the perfect candidate for the Great Experiment.

Rickey dispatched his scouts to find a player to break baseball's color barrier. It wouldn't be an easy task. The

Negro Leagues were full of tremendous stars with more than enough raw talent to play at the highest level. Josh Gibson, for example, was such a prolific power hitter that he was largely known as "the black Babe Ruth" (although Gibson preferred to call Babe Ruth 'the white Josh Gibson').

James "Cool Papa" Bell was a speedy outfielder fast enough to turn weak contact into base hits and steal bases at will. In one account of his speed, he was said to flip the light switch off in his room and be in bed, under the covers, before the room went dark. He was also known to play in very shallow center field, giving him the chance to back up any hits up the middle. When the ball was hit over his head, his raw speed allowed him to catch up to the ball and make the play.

And then there was Satchel Paige. Perhaps no other player in baseball history has more folklore or mythology surrounding their legacy than Leroy "Satchel" (or simply "Satch") Paige. His tall frame and deadly arm were a menace on the mound. So confident in his abilities, he reportedly would tell his fielders to vacate the diamond before striking out the side.

Jackie Robinson didn't have these unbelievable stories about his baseball abilities. While he was a four-sport athlete in college, baseball was low on his list compared to basketball, football, or track and field. However, baseball would become his first occupation after leaving the army.

He played shortstop for the Kansas City Monarchs, batting an impressive .387.

Robinson caught the attention of Rickey, who sent his best scout, Clyde Sukeforth (the same man who would later discover Roberto Clemente), to watch the Black player in action and meet with him. Sukeforth was impressed with the player's performance on the field, intelligence in conversation, and his distinct pride in his race. A few days later, Jackie Robinson was in Rickey's office.

The first meeting between the two forged an incredible partnership. Rickey tested Robinson's mettle, giving him every possible scenario that the Black player would experience. The deeply religious man hurled every insult and racial slur he could think of at Jackie, testing how thick his skin was, the very skin that had kept him and his race out of organized baseball for decades.

Rickey asked Robinson to promise that he would not retaliate to any abuse on or off the field for three years. He knew that even the smallest incident would derail any progress they made. The world, particularly the media, would look for any reason to demonize Jackie. Robinson thought about this promise, agreed, and the Great Experiment was underway.

Jackie's Game

The crafty Branch Rickey started Robinson's path to the Dodgers and professional baseball in Montreal, playing for the Royals. He thought Robinson would have an easier time playing in Canada because racism wasn't as prolific. Still, the player faced an ocean of criticism and outright bigotry. His own manager had made remarks that he didn't believe Robinson was a human being because he was black.

Robinson's skills quickly shone out, silencing many of these detractors. In his first game, he went four for five, stole two bases, and scored two runs. It was a great game with many more still to come. Ignoring every attempt from opposing players and fans to get a reaction from him, Robinson seemed to play better and better. His aggressive hitting, fielding, and baserunning drove the Royals all the way to victory in the Minor League World Series. The same manager that questioned Jackie's humanity had changed his tune, calling Robinson a great ballplayer.

With Jackie's success at the Montreal Royals, it became apparent to the Dodgers players that he would be joining the team soon. Several players created a petition, stating they'd rather be traded than share a dugout or clubhouse with a Black man. Leo Durocher, the Dodgers manager, called a meeting to put an end to the problem.

"I don't care if the guy is yellow or black or if he has stripes like a zebra. I'm the manager of this team and I say he plays…This guy don't come to the ballpark to beat you. He comes to beat you bad. This Robinson, he plays a ton," Durocher said. He went on to echo the fears that every petitioner felt. Robinson was coming and he was only the beginning. More black players would begin entering the big leagues, taking jobs from any white players who lacked the skills or drive to continue their baseball careers.

On April 15, 1947, Jackie Robinson jogged out of the dugout with his Dodger teammates and onto Ebbets Field. With each step across the diamond to his position at first base, baseball's longstanding color barrier crumbled. The event didn't just change Major League Baseball; it influenced America's perception of race and character.

Robinson wasn't just the first Black baseball player. He became as big a gate attraction as Babe Ruth, and it wasn't because of the color of his skin. It was because of how exciting he was to watch. His baserunning won the hearts of Dodgers fans, white and black.

Once he got on base, whether by a hit or a walk, every eye in the stadium fell on him as if he was center stage under a spotlight. It was unlike anything organized baseball had ever seen. Robinson would dance off the bag, an ever-present threat to steal. It ruined any pitcher's focus, forcing wild pitches and walks. Dodger fans loved it.

The home crowd enjoyed his electric play, but for Robinson, the big leagues were an unending nightmare. Every day tested his resolve and made him question his ability to keep his promise to Branch Rickey. He received threats on his life and the lives of his wife and child. Pitchers threw at his head. Fans and opposing players taunted him from the first to the final outs of the game.

It was all designed to break Robinson down until he snapped. Baseball owners, managers, fans, and players who wanted the game to remain White knew that's all it would take for Rickey and Robinson's "Great Experiment" to fail.

Whether the abuse Robinson endured was a concerted effort or not, the result became a positive force on the Brooklyn Dodgers. The turning point came against Philadelphia, one of the teams known for verbally bashing Jackie the most. Led by manager Ben Chapman, the Phillies' racial barrage got so out of control that Eddie Stanky, Robinson's teammate and one of the petitioners who threatened to quit if he joined the Dodgers, came to his defense. He demanded Chapman pick on someone who could fight back.

It was a sign that Robinson's teammates were behind him. They had watched game after game as Jackie took pitches to the head and spikes to his ankles. They had heard every insult and racial slur. They had seen a human being endure more than anyone ought to in a lifetime, let alone in a baseball season. The other members of the Dodgers could no longer sit idly by and watch their teammate receive all of this abuse. Their passion for protecting him became so hot one day that it was Robinson who had to talk the other players down from retaliating against the opposing team.

The Dodgers weren't the only entity to start coming around. *The Sporting News,* a publication that was openly opposed to integrating black people into organized baseball, was now awarding Robinson the first Rookie of the Year. More impressively, the black baseball player was voted the second most popular person in America.

Through his demeanor, resolve, and pure baseball talent, Jackie Robinson began to heighten the awareness of the American people on the evils of racism and the purity of equality. It matured the nation morally and began the conversations and questions that challenged the unfair systems in the country.

Robinson never fought back or returned any of the hatred so easily dispensed upon him because he had the entire black race on his shoulders. His actions in baseball progressed the entire nation, propelling it toward a brighter and more just future. The heroism he displayed (and there truly is no other word to use) is not only the single greatest achievement of an athlete but one of the great victories of Good over Evil within the human drama.

Every year on April 15, Major League Baseball remembers Jackie Robinson's achievements. Players across baseball wear his number 42 and take time to remember the sacrifices he made.

CONCLUSION

Baseball remains one of the hardest sports to play. The most successful players only hit roughly three out of every ten times at the plate, meaning baseball players fail more times than they succeed. Even baseball's best players and greatest teams face times when winning and success don't come easily. Only through hard work, determination, and an unwavering belief in themselves are they able to thrive and win.

Inspirational baseball stories, like the 12 included in these pages, are vital reminders that the worst slumps and biggest defeats are only temporary. If you leave this book with one lesson it is this:

Never shy away from a challenge.

The season that Ted Williams achieved his legendary .406 batting average, he had an opportunity to sit out the last few games and guarantee his .400+ season. For Williams, that was unacceptable. The record wouldn't have felt authentic if he sat on the bench and avoided his remaining at-bats. He stepped to the plate and made his permanent mark on baseball.

This echoes Ichiro's wisdom that giving your best effort is the most important thing. Records and awards are secondary and hollow if you achieve them without hard work. Was Derek Jeter satisfied being #7th in the country in high school? No, he pushed himself to become #1. He could have been happy with one World Series title. Instead, he led the New York Yankees to five.

Jim Abbott or Pete Gray could have given up on their dreams and blamed their physical handicaps, giving in to the people around them that told them they couldn't be big leaguers. Adam Greenberg could have taken a similar route and let his chance at his first MLB at-bat slip away.

What if the 2004 Red Sox gave up after losing the first three games to the Yankees in the ALCS, or the Marlins stopped their season once COVID-19 took out their best players? No one could have blamed them. They were facing impossible odds. Yet so was Jackie Robinson. What if he had given up?

Every person or team mentioned throughout this book had many chances to take the easy way out or give up entirely on their pursuits, even if just for the rest of the season. They didn't.

Inspiration is born out of impossibility becoming reality. No one is inspired by meeting expectations. If you always steer toward challenges, instead of away from them, you'll be an inspiring presence to yourself, your team, your peers, and anyone else around you.

Made in the USA
Coppell, TX
25 September 2023

21997995R00075